Physical Characteristics of the Puli

(from the American Kennel Club breed standard)

D1608558

DISCARDED

Back: Level and strong, of medium length, with croup sloping slightly.

Loin: Short, strong and moderately tucked up.

Tail: Carried over, and blends into the backline.

Hindquarters: Well developed and muscular with well bent stifles, the rear assembly balancing that of the front. The hocks are perpendicular to the ground and well let down. Feet as in front.

Coat: The outer coat is wavy or curly, but never silky. The undercoat is soft, woolly and dense. The coat clumps together easily, and if allowed to develop naturally, will form cords in the adult.

Color: Only the solid colors of rusty black, black, all shades of gray and white are acceptable.

Puli

◇

By Ann Arch

Nashville
Public Library
Foundation

*This book made possible
through a generous gift
from Robin and Bill King
to the Nashville Public Library
Foundation Book Fund*

Contents

Training Your Puli · 71

Begin with the basics of training the puppy and adult dog. Learn the principles of house-training the Puli, including the use of crates and basic scent instincts. Get started by introducing the pup to his collar and leash and progress to the basic commands. Find out about obedience classes and other activities.

Healthcare of Your Puli · 97

By Lowell Ackerman DVM, DACVD
Become your dog's healthcare advocate and a well-educated canine keeper. Select a skilled and able veterinarian. Discuss pet insurance, vaccinations and infectious diseases, the neuter/spay decision and a sensible, effective plan for parasite control, including fleas, ticks and worms. Also included is a special section on common eye diseases.

Your Senior Puli · 134

Know when to consider your Puli a senior and what special needs he will have. Learn to recognize the signs of aging in terms of physical and behavioral traits and what your vet can do to optimize your dog's golden years.

Showing Your Puli · 142

Step into the center ring and find out about the world of showing pure-bred dogs. Here's how to get started in AKC shows, how to prepare for the show ring and basic organization of conformation shows. Take a leap into the realms of obedience trials, agility trials, tracking tests and herding events.

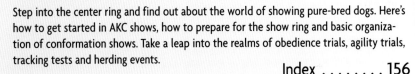

KENNEL CLUB BOOKS® PULI
ISBN: 1-59378-263-2

Copyright © 2006 • Kennel Club Books, LLC
308 Main Street, Allenhurst, NJ 07711 USA
Cover Design Patented: US 6,435,559 B2 • Printed in South Korea

All rights reserved. No part of this book may be reproduced in any form, by photostat, scanner, microfilm, xerography or any other means, or incorporated into any information retrieval system, electronic or mechanical, without the written permission of the copyright owner.

10 9 8 7 6 5 4 3 2 1

Photography by Michael Trafford
with additional photographs by:

Ann Arch, Ashbey Studios, Kim Booth, Paulette Braun, T.J. Calhoun, Carolina Biological Supply, Warren and Victoria Cook, Alexandra Davis, Isabelle Français, Carol Ann Johnson, Bill Jonas, Kernan Studios, Dr. Dennis Kunkel, Tam C. Nguyen, Phototake, Jean Claude Revy, Stewart Event Images, Ian and Karen Stewart and Missy Yuhl.

Illustrations by Renée Low and Patricia Peters.

Special thanks to Stephanie Horan for the US and Canadian history sections and to Prof. Dr. Robert L. Peiffer, Jr. for the eye disease section.

Pulik are seen in black, rusty-black, white and various shades of gray and apricot, but not all countries accept all colors. Whatever the color, it should be solid.

BREED DEVELOPMENT AND ESTABLISHMENT

The background of the Puli is certainly lengthy and quite romantic. Although we regard the breed as being of Hungarian background, research indicates origins farther east. When one compares the Puli with the Tibetan Terrier, for example, there are strong similarities. Moreover, the Tibetan breeds were not separated into varieties until about 75 years ago.

Research indicates the existence of Pulik as far back as the ninth century, in the region between the Don and Dnieper Rivers. However, when sites of even earlier ancient civilizations were excavated, remains very much resembling the Puli were found. These date back as far as 2500 BC. At Eridu, on the Euphrates River, where excavation revealed one of the oldest cities on earth, archaeologists found the tomb of an eight-year-old princess named Il-De. She was buried with many of her possessions, among which was a tiny 5-inch-tall alabaster statue of her little dog—clearly recognizable as a Puli! Believed to be around 4,500 years old, the statue was last recorded

Although associated with Hungary, the Puli's origin can be traced farther east. Similarities between the Puli and the Tibetan Terrier, shown here, are evident.

beyond the Aral Sea and invaded the Carpathian Basin. They were called White Huns, as well as Avars, and were thought to know the term "Puli." The word *puli*, which commonly refers to a drover, can still be heard in parts of India and other areas through which the Avars traveled. The Magyars lived for quite a while in the Don and Dnieper River basins where these nomadic horsemen adapted to hunting, fishing and trading. In time, they gradually spread into Transylvania, over the Carpathian Mountains, where they were recorded around AD 895 or 896. They took with them large herds of cattle and flocks of sheep. The sheep, related to the Ovis Ammon Polh, were known as Argali. This horned breed spread as far as Bokhara and into China. Longhaired sheepskins dating back to 500 and 400 BC were found in the frozen wastelands of the Altai region.

as being exhibited in the National Museum of Iraq in Baghdad.

Tribes of nomadic horsemen who ranged across Asia had been known to the ancient Chinese since around 1200 BC. They called them the Puli Hou or the Destroyer Hun. Traveling farther west, by the fifth century AD they had spread as far as Europe by way of the Danube River. These invaders rode with their herds and their unruly semi-wild dogs. In AD 453, after their leader Attila died, they retreated to Asia.

Hungary had experienced other invaders, and in AD 567 came the Avars, who eventually divided into tribes. One of the groups settled down and merged with the tribes of northern India while others moved westward on

The Magyars were a wild, hardy and rather fierce people who effectively drove out the earlier inhabitants of the wide Danube Valley where they then settled with their dogs. Although

THE PLURAL OF PULI
In Hungary, the plural of Puli is "Pulix," while in English-speaking countries the plural is "Pulik," though "Pulis" is also used.

the Puli was in Hungary by AD 899, there remained very similar dogs in the northern Himalayas.

Through the years, attacks were made by invaders on the settling Magyars, with the most serious onslaught by the Mongols, under Genghis Khan, in the 13th century. Having been successful over most of Asia, they tried to conquer parts of Europe, too. To them, the term *puli* or *buri* meant "destroyer." The native Hungarian population was quite depleted, and Germans later settled where the worst battles had taken place.

Inevitably, other animals were brought into Hungary, including Merino sheep and some herding dogs similar to the French Briard and Beauceron. In relief carvings of the 12th and 14th centuries, varying types of dogs were depicted. Some had prick ears and curled tails, while others had no tails and dropped ears.

Although the earliest verifiable recording of a Puli occurred in 1751 in a description of various hunting dogs, the Hungarians called the Puli and another native breed, the Pumi, "Juhasz-Kutyak" (shepherds' dogs). The Puli, as we know it today, came about by breeding to French and German shepherding breeds. In 1815, the Puli and the Pumi were scientifically classified as *Canis familiaris pomeranius*. In 1901 the Puli was renamed *Canis familiaris domesti-*

cus hungaricus. It was around that period that many countries decided to ensure the preservation of their native breeds. In the 20th century, with the separation of the Puli and Pumi, sometimes an odd

PUMI

Another herding dog of Hungary is called the Pumi. Crosses to the Puli contributed to the Pumi's development. This medium-sized dog possesses unique upright ears and a curly coat, which, although long and thick, does not have a tendency to cord. The Pumi is a cattle drover and excels as a watchdog. In Hungary, the Pumi is the dog seen around town, while the Puli is seen more in the country and plains.

pup or two in a Puli litter can resemble a Pumi or even a Mudi, another similar herding dog of Hungary, showing the comparatively recent split.

In the beginning of the 20th century, judges at dog shows were so uncertain of what they were seeking as the ideal at exhibitions that sometimes completely differing types were awarded prizes—prick-ears, short coats or pointed heads! Variations in size were also quite common in the first 30 or 40 years, as the early breed standard spoke of the Puli as "a medium-sized sheepdog." Prior to World War II, pictures showed the breed with quite long legs, coats often not in the now-familiar cords and with tails that were sometimes carried lower and not always over the back.

Though recorded in some detail as show dogs at early shows in Budapest, both the Puli and Pumi were termed as "Juhasz-Kutyak." To the shepherd, they were known as two distinct breeds and given their own titles. In his book *Working Dogs of the World* (1947), Clifford Hubbard (affectionately known to all canine enthusiasts in Britain as "Doggy" Hubbard) noted that the Puli was starting to become quite well known outside Hungary. Before World War II, Pulik were being bred in Austria, Germany and Italy, and American fanciers began to take an interest in the breed.

In Hungary, the organization formed to safeguard native sheepdog breeds had a very long name and became known by its initials: MEOE (Magyar Ebtenyéstők Országos Egyesülete). Set up in 1899, the MEOE kept all early records of breeding and standards for the breeds encompassed. The veterinarian attached to the Budapest Zoo, Dr. Emil Raitsits, was influential in many ways, and the first Puli breed standard was eventually published in 1915. It was improved in 1924, when it was accepted by the Fédération Cynologique Internationale (FCI), which is the "umbrella" canine organization to which the major-

A modern English-bred champion Puli from the Loakespark kennel.

ity of European countries belong. The FCI has extended its area of operation beyond Europe to many countries around the world.

Dr. Raitsits formed an alternative club in the early 1930s, but the FCI refused to recognize it. This club allowed for a variation in both size and color (including particolors). They were also prepared to accept for registration dogs that resembled the breed but had no paperwork to prove their origins. This confused not only the Hungarians but also people from other countries who, in good faith, purchased stock intended as foundation for setting up the breed overseas.

Following World War II, with the gene pool drastically reduced, showing and breeding resumed with quite strong jurisdiction over breeders by the MEOE. This organization was responsible for the first shows and encouraged quality stock among breeders and exhibitors. As the level was so high, the show attracted inquiries from many countries, especially the US and Britain. The British then exported stock to Australia and New Zealand.

The first mention of a Puli in England involved Clive of India, who was bartered from a German ex-serviceman by a Miss Turpin of Stafford for 20 Players cigarettes. He was shown at a Stafford Canine Society Show around

1950. The breed gained strength when the Ingus family lived in London for a while before going on to America. In 1967 they arrived in London with their pet Puli Bodri. In 1969 they imported a bitch in whelp to the world-famous Int. Ch. Pusztai Furtos Ficko. Hungarian Ch. Kiscellehegyi Furge Csopi whelped four puppies in quarantine. As with all quarantine-born puppies, they were released as soon as they had been weaned, leaving their mother to complete her six months. At a show held by the Hammersmith Canine Society in 1970, Mr. Ingus showed Bodri, and his floor-length corded coat attracted a great deal of attention. He and the puppies were subsequently featured in the national press and on television, where they aroused

The Beauceron is a French shepherd dog that many believe was used in the development of the Puli in Hungary.

The Mudi is another Hungarian herding dog similar to the Puli and Pumi; it is said that an occasional Puli pup can resemble a Mudi.

THE PULI IN THE UNITED STATES

By Stephanie Horan

When the US Department of Agriculture (USDA) determined in the 1930s that the herding dogs currently in use needed some improvement, they looked to Hungary for the solution. Many of the American dogs were vicious and often they injured or even killed the animals they were supposed to protect. The USDA heard that the Puli, a Hungarian sheepdog breed, was reputed to be intelligent as well as much gentler with the livestock. Thus, in 1935 four Pulik were imported into the USDA's facilities in Beltsville, Maryland. These dogs were bred and were also crossed with German Shepherds, Border Collies, Chow Chows and some Turkish sheepdogs. The dogs were tested at various ages for their herding abilities, but the outbreak of World War II stopped this experiment. The results were inconclusive, and no official report was compiled, but scattered anecdotes describing how the Pulik impressed some of the veterinarians involved have come down through the years. The dogs were all sold.

The American Kennel Club (AKC) recognized the breed in 1936, and the first to be registered was owned by Louis Kiss of Marlboro, New York. He and Bronson

even more interest in this unusual breed. The Ingus family then moved to the US in 1971.

Of the four puppies, one went to Pat Lanz, already very well known for her Rottweilers under her Borgvaale affix. A dog named Immerzu went to Mr. and Mrs. Terry Horan, who later emigrated to Canada, while the remaining dog and bitch went to Nancy and Mike Tomlin, who had pioneered the Briard in the British show ring. Later, imports were brought in by Mrs. Lanz and by Mrs. Stretton, who had become interested in the Puli while her husband was working in Germany. Mrs. Stretton's linguistic ability facilitated her dealings with the Hungarian breeders.

Williams of Frenchtown, New Jersey are known to have obtained stock from the dispersal of the dogs at the Beltsville facility. However, it was Nicholas Roosevelt—writer, soldier and diplomat—who raised America's awareness of the breed when he brought two Pulik home with him after spending two years in Hungary as US Ambassador. After he retired to California, his family continued to have Pulik in their lives for many years.

The Puli remained a comparatively rare breed until the late 1940s. It was then that a two-year-old bitch named Juli II, bred by Bronson Williams, fortuitously came into the ownership of Schuyler and Sylvia Owen of Hope, New Jersey. Juli became the foundation of the Skysyl Puli kennel, and Sylvia embarked on a campaign to put the Puli breed prominently in the public eye. She helped start the Puli Club of America (PCA) in 1951 and was its first secretary. She wrote magazine articles and also the book *The Complete Puli* and was unstinting in her efforts over the years to bring attention to the breed she loved. The Skysyl dogs were known for their brushed coats, at the time an acceptable style in the show ring in the US, which Sylvia much preferred.

Mrs. Owen bred the first Best in Show Puli: Ch. Skysyl Question Being Is It, who won the

CORDED COATS

The Puli is not unique in the world of dogs for its cords. Corded coats occur on other pure-bred dogs including the Komondor (ABOVE), a giant white Hungarian guard dog. The Italian equivalent to the Puli is the Bergamasco (BELOW), a corded herder that comes in shades of gray, black and tan. Perhaps the most popular dog in the world that may be seen in cords is the Poodle, though this coat fashion has a very small following in the Poodle world today.

Ch. Kallopusztai Apor with his breeder/handler Vilma Majores, gaiting around the group ring.

Gray, who was campaigned very successfully in the late '50s into the early '60s, and won the national specialty a record total of five times. Many of the Cedwood Pulis were gray.

Both Cedwood and Skysyl dogs became the foundation of the Gooseberry Hill kennel in Wisconsin. Started in 1956 by Mr. and Mrs. John B. McManus, the kennel continues to this day under the name of their eldest daughter, Susan McManus Maas. As well as several winning dogs carrying the Gooseberry Hill name, Ch. Pulikountry's Apro CD, bred by Robert and Anne Kennedy, became a Best in Show winner in 1971 under the ownership of Gooseberry Hill. He was the first male Puli to win BIS, and also the first in a corded coat.

trophy in 1968. Skysyl produced several other Best in Show (BIS) and specialty winners, one of the most famous being Ch. Skysyl Harvey J. Wallbanger, who was also a top producer with 48 champion get. Ann Bowley handled the Skysyl dogs for many years, and they formed the basis for her Wallbanger Pulik, of whom the fabulous Ch. Wallbanger Kermit J. Bounce was Herding Group winner at the Westminster Kennel Club Dog Show in 1989, and also garnered an impressive 26 BIS awards during his show career.

Ellanor Anderson of Bristol, Connecticut began her Cedwood kennel in 1954, and much of her stock descended from Skysyl bloodlines. Her most prominent dog was Ch. Cedwood's Anthony

In 1963 the AKC added the Hungarian Kennel Club (MEOE) to its list of recognized registries, and imports of Hungarian dogs began. A great deal of dissension rose when the imports were seen to be quite different from the American-bred dogs with regard to size, type, color and coat. Before this time, American breeders and exhibitors had been able to obtain very little information regarding the Puli from its native land, and some felt that the breed was now far removed from the Hungarian ideal and had fallen into a state of lethargy in the US. The new imports and their

Ch. Pulikountry's Apro, CD, owned by Mrs. John B. McManus.

descendants began to do some serious winning in the show rings. A turf war erupted and continued for many years, much of it centered on the so-called "American" Pulik with their brushed-out coats and the corded coats of the newcomers, which the older established breeders disliked.

Leslie and Klara Benis of Tarzana, California were important Puli breeders in the 1960s and '70s with their Hunnia kennel. They had emigrated to the US from Hungary, where Les had grown up with the breed, and he campaigned many Hungarian imports in immaculate corded coats to dispel the myth of the "smelly" and "dirty" cords. Hunnia's most famous Puli was the exquisite BIS-winning bitch Ch. Sasvolgyi Puszi Pajtas, bred in Hungary by Les. He is one of the most respected experts in the breed and is the author of *This Is the Puli*.

Barbara Edwards and Constance Peterson started their Prydain kennel in 1974 in California and contributed much with their top-winning Pulik in both conformation and performance events. They produced several BIS- and specialty-winning dogs, with Ch. Prydain Noah and Ch. Prydain Trademark HT being outstanding examples. Prydain also owned an exceptional dam in Ch. Prydain Virag HT, who produced 30 champion get, 2 of whom became multi-BIS winners.

The top-producing Puli in North America is a Hungarian import, Ch. Csanyteleki Csigany, owned by Terry and Mary Wakeman of Connecticut. He has sired 52 champions and, despite being owner-handled over a fairly short show career, he also won 6 BIS awards and the national specialty twice, in 1984 and 1985.

THE PULI IN CANADA
By Stephanie Horan

The first Puli in Canada was a German-bred dog, Ch. Adolar von der Herlingsberg CDX, who accompanied his owner Mrs. R.D. McLellan when she moved from Germany to Montreal in 1948. Mrs. McLellan helped to found a club encompassing all of the Hungarian breeds. In addition to being the club's secretary, she was the club's newsletter editor and succeeded in persuading many prominent Puli experts to contribute articles to the publication.

The history of the Puli in Canada was somewhat patchy for many years, with no really prominent dogs or breeders, just the occasional dog or owner doing quite well for a short time but then disappearing without making any lasting contribution. This guest author and husband Terry Horan emigrated to Canada from the UK in 1974, bringing their Immerzu Pulik, and have played a key role in the Canadian Puli world with many champions, group winners and top producers. They helped to start the Puli Club of Alberta in 1975, which was renamed Puli Club of Canada a few years later to reflect the growing national interest in the club.

A handful of Pulik have won Bests in Show in Canada. These were all imports or owned by visiting American exhibitors until 1999, when Ch. Kirasdream Anji of Immerzu became the first Canadian-bred Puli, and also the first bitch, to take that honor. She was owned by Ann Tober of Edmonton, Alberta. Bernie and Bobbie Silverman of Toronto have owned two multi-BIS-winning Pulik in recent years, Ch. Fuzzy Farm Csibesz Checker, an American-bred male, and Ch. Kalacsos Muci, a white Hungarian-bred bitch.

The Puli remains a comparatively rare breed in both the US and Canada, but has a loyal and devoted following determined to keep this unique breed a sound and eye-catching little sheepdog.

CHARACTERISTICS OF THE

PULI

The Puli is a lively and extremely intelligent breed. The breed loves to be a part of family life and particularly resents being ignored or only being included "when convenient." The dog will live quite happily both as a single dog and, providing that integration is carefully effected, will also be content as one of several. As a breed that was worked all the time, it has the stamina to perform its duties around the clock, every single day, so it is not really suited to a dull routine without exercise or other activity. As a family dog, it is ideal, always willing to play with the children and with a fun outlook on life. The Puli has the added value of acting as an effective warning instrument if strangers approach, as the breed has excellent hearing. Again, Pulik thoroughly enjoy participating in family activities, particularly whole days out with walking and romping about. We find that ours love to do some simple basic obedience—going to "fetch" being the earliest. A favorite for such retrieves is a short length of hardwearing rope that is knotted at both ends. When Pulik compete seriously in obedience competition, they require a much smaller dumbbell than the normal size. Pulik have competed with success in obedience and agility, and they now also frequently compete with other breeds in herding trials.

Perhaps the one thing that sets the breed apart and makes it so special is its coat. The Puli is born with a smooth and quite dense covering. This jacket soon starts to grow and will continue to grow longer and longer throughout the dog's entire life.

The corded Puli jacket is quite distinctive, and Puli owners are

Pulik are extremely intelligent and playful dogs.

delighted to have such an attractive, unique breed. However, there may be circumstances when it is impossible to maintain such a coat. They can be clipped down, or perhaps the cords reduced to a few inches in length. Keeping the mature jacket in full show condition is quite an undertaking, and those with several Pulik to cope with will often clip the coats on those that are no longer being exhibited. It is far better that you keep a Puli clean and sweet-smelling rather than retain a long coat that is untended and dirty. The coat serves as natural insulation, being capable of keeping the animal warm and dry, and stopping the sun from reaching and burning the skin. In the warmer weather, we clip off the coat under the belly, from behind the elbow, right along the rib cage and the belly, and on to the insides of the tops of the hindlegs. When it's

The Puli is a true family dog—he loves to be part of his owners' lives, he adapts well to almost any living situation, and he fares well in a single- or multi-dog household.

warm, Pulik tend to sleep on their backs so that they stay cooler.

The Puli's unusual coat needs particular attention if it is to be maintained in good condition. For example, the Puli should never be left outdoors in all types of weather. If the dog is to spend time outdoors in a run, a portion should be covered, in case of rain, to prevent water from soaking the dog's coat, as it will take quite a while to dry. If left wet, it can soon become smelly and offensive to all.

Quite tough in their constitution, Pulik are easy to feed, not requiring exotic or high-protein meals. After all, they would have had little chance to enjoy the high protein in meat, as they were living with nomad shepherds and making do with whatever scraps were thrown to them. The Puli is a wiry, fine-boned dog. Any extra weight would only slow down the animal and, in time, put a strain on his heart and lungs. It is the easiest breed we have ever owned, not only for its general health but also for house-training. As long as a regular routine is established early, Pulik are soon trustworthy around the house.

What type of home is best? Pulik adapt to wherever their families live. Apartment dwellers can cope very well with the breed as long as they follow a regular exercise routine.

From the time that the Puli arrives in his new home, you must

remember that you have an ultra-intelligent animal living with you. There is an old saying, "A Puli is not a dog. A Puli is a Puli." This sums up the breed's distinctive character very well! Pulik are very much like active and intelligent children who respond well to sensible discipline. As long as they learn what is expected of them as soon as possible, they soon become well-behaved members of the household. From the time they arrive and become accustomed to their new surroundings, it takes a very short time for them to adjust to your routine.

Feeding and exercising your Puli should be carried out at regular times, which helps him to develop a sense of security. It is also important that if your dog is to be taken out and about in a car, he should begin with some preliminary short trips. Early forays may cause a little carsickness, or he may be tempted to start jumping around. For this

The Puli is one of the few corded breeds in dogdom; this type of coat is very distinctive and requires maintenance.

reason, we definitely recommend a travel crate. A crated Puli will be safe during car trips and will also feel right at home, as you should be utilizing the crate as part of his house-training.

In the early weeks of bringing your puppy home, you will certainly limit his access around the house as he is being house-trained, learning the house rules and getting accustomed to his crate. The author's dogs, as they've grown up, have eventually been given full run of the house, as Pulik tend to be well-behaved indoors. This is possible with a well-trained adult; use your judgment based on your individual dog. Regardless, it is

Originally bred as herding dogs with the stamina to work all day, the Puli is a very active dog with superior intelligence. He needs exercise and activities done with his owners.

This is why people have dogs as pets—the dog/owner bond is priceless.

always beneficial to crate-train from puppyhood so that the dog will be comfortable in his crate and you can use the crate when needed. No matter how well-behaved the pup or adult, you must always dog-proof the areas to which he has access.

Caring breeders will only breed from stock that has been screened, through official means, for any known hereditary problems. People may be concerned at the mention of such problems, for there are known to be about 300 identified hereditary problems in the dog world, but the number of currently identified hereditary defects in the human world is over 1000! This surely puts it into perspective. In the Puli it is customary to have hips x-rayed, which is done in most breeds. Dogs 24 months of age and older should have their hips x-rayed and the x-rays evaluated by the Ortho-

The Puli is a naturally athletic and agile dog. Ch. Loakespark Just Smart, NAJ is one leaping Puli, owned by A. Davis and C. Nusbickel.

pedic Foundation for Animals (OFA) to determine if any degree of dysplasia is present. A dog younger than 24 months cannot be certified as free of dysplasia. Upon the x-rays' examination by a panel of vets, there are seven possible grades for a dog's hips: Excellent, Good, Fair, Borderline, Mild, Moderate and Severe. Excellent, Good and Fair are considered normal, and dogs with these gradings will receive an OFA number. The other four gradings do not warrant an OFA number, with the latter three indicating that the dog is affected by some level of dysplasia. Dogs that do not receive OFA numbers should not be used in breeding programs.

PULI

Following is the breed standard for the Puli as approved by the American Kennel Club, with the author's comments following in italics.

THE AMERICAN KENNEL CLUB STANDARD FOR THE PULI

General Appearance: The Puli is a compact, square appearing, well balanced dog of medium size. He is vigorous, alert and active. Striking and highly characteristic is the shaggy coat which, combined with his light-footed, distinctive movement, has fitted him for the strenuous work of herding flocks on the plains of Hungary. Agility, combined with soundness of mind and body, is of prime importance for the proper fulfillment of this centuries-old task.

It's quite a surprise, on first handling a Puli, to find under the enormous mature corded coat, a lean, hard, conditioned, fine-boned and very wiry little animal. When you observe from the side and visualize the body and limbs minus the neck and head, they should approximate a square.

Size, Proportion, Substance: Ideally, males are 17 inches measured from the withers to the ground; bitches, 16 inches. An inch over or under these measurements is acceptable. The tightly knit body approximates a square measured from withers to ground and point of shoulder to point of buttock. Medium boned.

As a judge, when seeking breed type, balance and soundness, it can be difficult to make decisions that are understood by all. Size is important; for example, oversize is undesirable as it can lead to coarseness. However,

The quality of a Puli for show purposes is evaluated according to the official breed standard.

Here's what quality looks like: Ch. Cordmaker Mississippi Mud was the number-one Puli in the US for four years from 1999 to 2002 and placed among the top Herding Dogs each year. He is shown with handler Linda Pitts.

Head: The *head* is of medium size in proportion to the body. The almond shaped *eyes* are deep set, rather large and dark brown with black or slate gray eye rims. The *ears,* set on somewhat higher than the level of the eyes, are hanging, of medium size, V-shape and about half the head length. The *skull* slightly domed and medium broad. The *stop* is defined, but not abrupt. The *muzzle* is strong and straight, a third of the head length, and ends in a nose of good size. The *nose* is always black. Flews and gums are black or slate gray. Flews are tight. A full complement of *teeth,* comparatively large, meet in a scissors bite.

The head of the Puli is very special. Under no circumstances should judges ignore the call for correct size, proportions and fineness, coupled with the domed skull. The skull-muzzle ratios of two-thirds to one-third is of great importance, for a too lengthy muzzle immediately suggests coarseness. The lack of dome on the skull will also lead to an impression of coarseness. The need for a relatively large nose is understandable in any working animal that needs to produce a turn of speed or enduring gait, when they will require unimpeded inhalation of air quickly into the lungs.

type and balance are also very important. It is difficult for a judge to give an award to an animal that falls within specified size ranges but lacks breed type or balance. The word "type" is frequently used but is far from easy to describe. My own interpretation is that "type" is what makes a breed special and identifiable, apart from others with similarities. If we didn't have "breed type" then all similar breeds could eventually end up very much alike.

The description of the eyes should apply to all colors, and

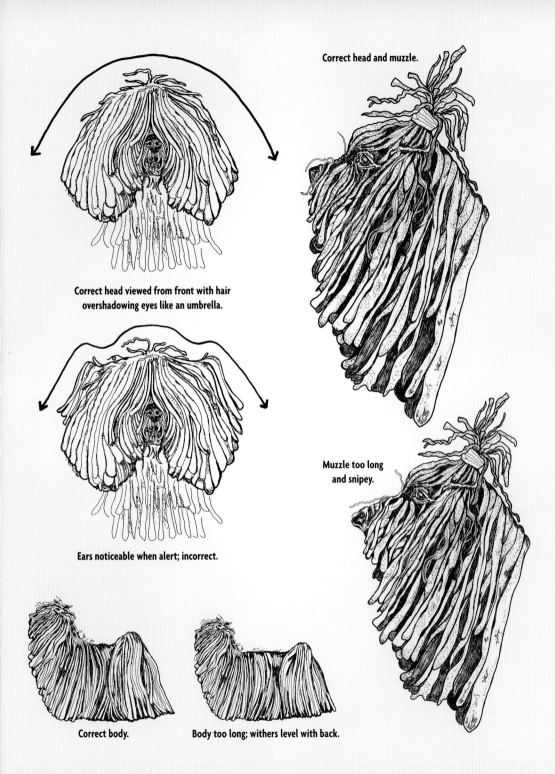

Correct head and muzzle.

Correct head viewed from front with hair
overshadowing eyes like an umbrella.

Ears noticeable when alert; incorrect.

Muzzle too long
and snipey.

Correct body.

Body too long; withers level with back.

Dark brown eyes with well-pigmented eye rims are typical in all coat colors, according to the standard.

Neck: There can be no doubt as to the requirement. Perhaps some judges may be influenced into believing that a longer neck is better—some have even gone as far as to praise a "good reachy neck"—but that is quite incorrect. The top of the head, when viewed from the side, is only a little higher than the top arch of the tail, giving a balanced appearance.

Body: This is described very well, and due to the very abundant coat in the mature Puli, the body must be checked carefully by a "hands-on" examination.

Tail: In some youngsters, when excited, the tail may be held a fraction loose. This can also indicate a degree of apprehension when the dogs first enter the show ring. In mature dogs, the tail should be carried firmly.

eye rims should always be well pigmented. In a dog that will be out working at times in intense sunlight, lack of pigment could allow the skin to become burnt.

Neck, Topline, Body: The *neck* is strong, muscular, of medium length and free of throatiness. The *back* is level and strong, of medium length, with croup sloping slightly. The *chest* is moderately broad and deep—the ribs well sprung. The *loin* is short, strong and moderately tucked up. The *tail* is carried over, and blends into the backline.

Forequarters: The shoulders are well laid back. Upper arm and scapula are approximately equal in length and form an angle of 90 degrees. The forelegs are straight, strong and medium boned with strong and flexible pasterns. Dewclaws, if any, may be removed. The round, compact *feet* have well arched toes and thick cushioned pads. The Puli stands well up on his pads. The pads and nails are black or slate gray.

A real understanding of the dog and his working needs is

essential in order to fully appreciate correct forequarter construction. A good shoulder is essential in an animal that must be capable of bursts of strong and agile action. Working animals, dealing with quick-witted and cunning farm animals, must have the strength and ability to turn quickly. Without correct angulation, and the balance of the two main bones that make up the shoulder, clean forward reach and the ability to maintain untiring action are impeded if unbalanced. Most breeds will have a reasonable length and angulation of the bone that goes back from the forechest and up to the withers (scapula). However, a fairly common fault in so many breeds can be shortness or lack of angulation of what is called the "upper arm" (the bone that goes from the forechest back down to the elbow). If there is a lack of angulation in the shoulder, then the animal will be restricted in the length of forward reach it can attain. In turn, this will require a lot of tiny steps to cover a length of ground. An animal with better angulation will not need to take so many steps to cover the same distance, resulting in a less tired dog. Elbows should fit in neatly under the rib cage, and not be loose. This ensures strong and quite straight action when viewed from the front, without too much width between the legs.

Feet: This very important part of the dog should be checked carefully, for if the dog is to do a day's work, it is essential that feet should not be spread or have thin pads.

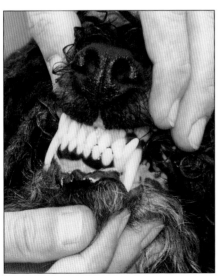

Hindquarters: The hindquarters are well developed and muscular with well bent stifles, the rear assembly balancing that of the front. The hocks are perpendicular to the ground and well let down. Dewclaws, if any, may be removed. Feet as in front.

This compares well to the need for forehand angulation. The standard mentions fairly low-set hocks and the actual joint should be checked for strength to ensure that there is no subluxation (sloping forward, rather like a double joint).

Jaws of the Puli are strong, and teeth should meet in a perfect scissors bite as shown.

Coat: The dense, weather resistant coat is profuse on all parts of the body. The outer coat is wavy or curly, but never silky. The undercoat is soft, woolly and dense. The coat clumps together easily, and if allowed to develop naturally, will form cords in the adult. The cords are wooly, varying in shape and thickness, either flat or round, depending on the texture of the coat and the balance of undercoat to outer coat. The Puli may be shown either corded or brushed. It is essential that the proper double coat with correct texture always be apparent. With age the coat can become quite long, even reaching to the ground; however, only enough length to properly evaluate quality and texture is considered necessary so as not to penalize the younger or working specimens.

Although all Pulik may look alike to the casual viewer, there is variety in the coat types that are possible. We once had a litter of four, all ending up with different types of cords in maturity. You may have the fine, rounded cord; the thicker and not-so-tight but still rounded cord; the flat "ribbon" type that can be quite hard or perhaps slightly softer and loose in its composition; or the occasional cord that appears to be composed of both felt and a little softer texture, which are usually slower in forming. Whatever type of cord starts to form, it is inadvisable to attempt to change it.

Color: Only the solid colors of rusty black, black, all shades of gray and white are acceptable; however, on the chest a white spot of not more than 2 inches is

Correct tail.

Incorrect tail; it should not appear separate from rump.

Incorrect tail set; too low.

There are various accepted coat colors in the Puli. Some colors may have black or white hairs intermingled, but the importance is the overall appearance of a solid color.

permissible. In the black and the gray dogs an intermixture of some gray, black or white hairs is acceptable as long as the overall appearance of a solid color is maintained. The fully pigmented skin has a bluish or gray cast whatever the coat color.

Not all colors are acceptable in all countries. In the UK, for example, shades of apricot are also accepted. Having seen and judged genetically pure whites, it is quite impressive to observe their solid black pigment on the nose, eye rims, flews, pads and nails, and all with quite a good slate-colored skin. Some that are registered as "white" can in later life be seen to have lost the important pigmentation, and this would be severely penalized by judges in FCI countries. The foregoing remarks also apply to some which have been classed as apricot. Hungary has never altered its pigment requirements.

Recognized in some places is the coloration "Facko." This is likened to an intermingling of gray and apricot, and will carry good pigmentation. Our original bitch was born and first registered as gray, but before she was old enough to exhibit, she turned apricot and her registration details were altered. As a black-masked apricot with excellent pigment, she became the UK's first (and only) apricot champion. However, in later life, the growth of gray coat could not be ignored, and we believe that she could have been termed "Facko." As it was, she produced some very good grays and started off a line that still favors that color.

Gait: The Puli is typically a lively, acrobatic dog; light, quick, agile and able to change directions instantly. At a collected, or contained trot the gait is distinctive: quick-stepping and animated, not far reaching, yet in no way mincing or stilted. When at a full trot, the Puli covers ground smoothly and efficiently with good reach and drive, the feet naturally tending to converge toward a median line of travel as speed increases. His distinctive movement is essential to the Puli's herding style.

All too often there is confusion over interpretation of this section of the standard. The Puli must have the capability for quick and sudden turns when required, and this would be impossible if the dog were to lack shoulder and hind angulation. The movement should have a light spring to it, and that is brought about by what can best be compared to the suspension of a car. If you don't have good suspension in your car, then every bump or uneven surface over which you travel will result in shock waves traveling upward. In a car, the passengers soon become uncomfortable; in similar fashion, the dog would soon become tired. Moreover, it is likely that in order to get quickly around to the other side of a flock, the Puli will spring up and run over the backs of sheep. This would be a struggle, if not impossible, if the angulations were lacking, thus preventing the agile, light, upward spring.

Temperament: By nature an affectionate, intelligent and home-loving companion, the Puli is sensibly suspicious and therefore an excellent watchdog. Extreme timidity or shyness are serious faults.

That they are wary of strangers is indicated by an unwillingness to launch themselves on visitors. We always advise anyone unknown to our dogs that he should start off by ignoring them. In a short time, an inquisitive little Hungarian will approach them, as Pulik are certainly curious.

Faults: Any deviation from the foregoing should be considered a fault, the seriousness of the fault depending upon the extent of the deviation.

Approved February 12, 1983
Reformatted June 19, 1990

PULI

CHOOSING AND REARING YOUR PULI PUPPY

As breeders, we have always found newborn Puli puppies to be really very contented little dears. We always think that they are rather like fat little slugs at the beginning. All they want is to feed and sleep. However, the time comes when they start to move around and develop personalities. We think Puli babies are born intelligent, compared to other breeds we have owned. At birth, one of ours, even before being expelled from his mother, was reaching round and trying to suckle. As soon as they are able, they'll start to crawl around with quite amazing determination. Even the opening of the eyes seems to be very early.

Most Puli pups are quite inquisitive and bold, so the choice of pup cannot be decided by which one is the outgoing character. Depending on whether you wish to show your Puli or keep him as a pet, it is best to be guided in your choice by the breeder or to take along an experienced friend, as the task of choosing is not easy. One would expect a price difference between the pup that appears to be a show prospect and the pup that may have some point that would make

HEALTH CLEARANCES

When visiting a litter, a potential owner should ask to see documentation of the litter's parents' hip clearances from OFA or another accredited organization; similar hip-testing programs are in place in countries around the world. Good breeders have all of their breeding stock tested and only breed from those dogs and bitches who have received appropriate clearances.

Before breeding, breeders must also make sure that both the bitch and the stud dog have appropriate clearances for hereditary eye diseases.

Resulting puppies should be eye screened as a whole litter prior to dispersal to their new homes. This is best done at seven to eight weeks of age. Any conscientious breeder will willingly produce copies of hip and eye documentation for prospective puppy purchasers from the Orthopedic Foundation for Animals (OFA) and the Canine Eye Registration Foundation (CERF). Also ask your breeder if he has done any testing for hearing defects.

him not quite so desirable for exhibition. For example, if a pup has a large flash of white, which will probably not disappear as the puppy grows, that Puli will still make a super family pet but would not have show potential, as only a small (2 inches or less) spot of white on the chest is acceptable in the show ring. We

MEET THE PARENTS

Because puppies are a combination of genes inherited from both of their parents, they will reflect the qualities and temperament of their sire and dam. When visiting a litter of pups, spend time with the dam and observe her behavior with her puppies, the breeder and with strangers. The sire is often not on the premises, but the dam should be with her pups until they are about eight weeks old. If either parent is surly, quarrelsome or fearful, it's likely that some of the pups will inherit those tendencies.

have found that in scrutinizing puppies in the first 36 to 48 hours following birth, it was possible to assess bone and body proportions, overall balance and construction before the well-fed puppy started to gain weight.

Caring breeders will have bred from a fit and healthy bitch and will do everything possible to ensure that the litter thrives. Sensible pre-natal feeding of the mother will continue after she whelps so that all possible good- ness passes through her milk into the whelps. As soon as they are ready for weaning, we have found that the most forward of our pups will attempt to join mom at her food dish. The youngsters will gradually go on to suitable quality nutrition, so that by the time you collect your new pup he will have received the best possible care. Breeders will also have wormed the litter prior to your collecting your new addition.

How do you go about finding a breeder? The national club for the breed, the Puli Club of America (PCA) can be found online at www.puliclub.org and offers breeder contact information so you can find the breeders in your region of the country. This is a trusted source for breeder referral, as PCA member breeders are obliged to follow the club's guide- lines in their breeding programs, ensuring that certain ethics and standards of care are met. It's up to you to contact these breeders, set up visits and decide with whom you are most comfortable. When you visit a breeder, ask to see all of his dogs (in addition to the litter, dam and possibly sire), observe the premises, see health documents on the parents (and pups where applicable), review pedigrees, read the breeder's sales contract, etc. The breeder will also have many questions for you to determine if you are a worthy owner of the breed; he will not agree to sell you a puppy unless he is sure that you can provide a wonderful home. Also be prepared to wait for an available litter and pup, as this is not a numerous breed.

Before the important day arrives, you will have made inquiries as to what foods and accessories you should have ready, such as a crate, toys, grooming tools, food dish, water

CREATE A SCHEDULE
Puppies thrive on sameness and routine. Offer meals at the same time each day, take him out at regular times for potty trips and do the same for play periods and outdoor activity. Make note of when your puppy naps and when he is most lively and energetic, and try to plan his day around those times. Once he is house-trained and more predictable in his habits, he will be better able to tolerate changes in his schedule.

bowl, etc. Don't spend a great deal of money on a tiny bed or crate, as puppies grow quite fast and by the time you have an adult in full coat, he will certainly need some-thing larger than he did at eight weeks of age. We advise that if owners want to get a dog bed, they should start off with an adult-sized one and put a smaller shallow cardboard box inside so that the puppy has something cozy to curl up in. The same goes for a crate, which can be parti-tioned into a puppy-sized area with a removable divider panel.

Do keep in touch with your breeder, for he will care about the welfare and the future of the puppies he has so carefully reared and will be eager to learn of your progress. He will be the best source of help and advice if you have queries or problems. The caring breeder will have carefully evaluated you as a prospective owner, especially if you have no previous experience. Be under-

When introduced to other dogs properly, Pulik do well in multiple-dog households. This owner has a small Hungarian herd.

standing as to his concern over the puppy's future and don't be upset by his questions and expectations. The breeder should ask you to sign some type of sales agreement (contract). You should not be surprised to be asked to agree that if for any reason you are unable to keep the puppy (or, later, the adult dog) you will first

> ### SELECTING FROM THE LITTER
> Before you visit a litter of puppies, promise yourself that you won't fall for the first pretty face you see! Decide on your goals for your puppy—show prospect, obedience competitor, family companion—and then look for a puppy who displays the appropriate qualities. In most litters, there is an alpha pup (the bossy puppy), and occasionally a shy fellow who is less confident, with the rest of the litter falling somewhere in the middle. "Middle-of-the-roaders" are safe bets for most families and novice competitors.

inform the breeder so that he can either take the dog back or be involved in the dog's rehoming. We should all feel responsible for anything that we breed, from the day it is born until the day it dies. Most Puli clubs have rescue committees to help rehome members of the breed, but the breeder of your dog is the person you should contact first in extenuating circumstances.

YOUR PULI SHOPPING LIST

Just as expectant parents prepare a nursery for their baby, so should you ready your home for the arrival of your Puli pup. If you have the necessary puppy supplies purchased and in place before he comes home, it will ease the puppy's transition from the warmth and familiarity of his mom and littermates to the brand-new environment of his new home and human family. You will be too busy to stock up and prepare your house after your pup comes home, that's for sure! Imagine how a pup must feel upon being transported to a strange new place. It's up to you to comfort him and to let your little pup know that he is going to be happy with you.

FOOD AND WATER BOWLS

Your puppy will need separate bowls for his food and water. Stainless steel pans are generally preferred over plastic bowls since they sterilize better and pups are less inclined to chew on the metal. Heavy-duty ceramic bowls are popular, but consider how often you will have to pick up those heavy bowls. Buy adult-sized pans, as your puppy will grow into them quickly.

THE DOG CRATE

If you think that crates are tools of punishment and confinement for when a dog has misbehaved, think again. Most breeders and almost all trainers recommend a crate as the preferred house-training aid as well as for all-around puppy training and safety. Because dogs are natural den creatures that prefer cave-like environments, the benefits of

The three most popular crate types: mesh on the left, wire on the right and fiberglass on top.

crate use are many. The crate provides the puppy with his very own "safe house," a cozy place to sleep, take a break or seek comfort with a favorite toy; a travel aid to house your dog when on the road, at motels or at the vet's office; a training aid to help teach your puppy proper toileting habits; and a place of solitude when non-dog people happen to drop by and don't want a lively puppy—or even a well-behaved adult dog—saying hello or begging for attention.

Crates come in several types, although the wire crate and the fiberglass airline-type crate are the most popular. The wire crates offer better visibility for the pup as well as better ventilation. Many of the

SOME DAM ATTITUDE

When selecting a puppy, be certain to meet the dam of the litter. The temperament of the dam is often predictive of the temperament of her puppies. However, dams occasionally are very protective of their young, some to the point of being testy or aggressive with visitors, whom they may view as a danger to their babies. Such attitudes are more common when the pups are very young and still nursing and should not be mistaken for actual aggressive temperament. If possible, visit the dam away from her pups to make friends with her and gain a better understanding of her true personality.

You should have acquired a crate before you brought your new Puli puppy home. Both you and your pup will appreciate the many benefits of crate-training.

wire crates easily fold into suitcase-size carriers. The fiberglass crates, similar to those used by the airlines for animal transport, are sturdier and more den-like. However, the fiberglass crates do not fold down and are less ventilated than wire crates, which can be problematic in hot weather. Some of the newer crates are made of heavy plastic mesh; they are very lightweight and fold up into slim-line suit-cases. However, a mesh crate might not be suitable for a pup with manic chewing habits.

At our home, Puli babies are introduced to wire crates at an early age. There is always a crate around for the pups, with its door left open. They can walk in and out, curl up on the bedding and accept the crate as part of their everyday surroundings. As it is always there, it holds no terror. We also find it helpful to feed the pups inside the crate at times, so they only associate the crate with pleasure. When they

SIGNS OF A HEALTHY PUPPY

Healthy puppies are robust little fellows who are alert and active, sporting shiny coats and supple skin. They should not appear lethargic, bloated or pot-bellied, nor should they have flaky skin or runny or crusted eyes or noses. Their stools should be firm and well formed, with no evidence of blood or mucus.

COST OF OWNERSHIP
The purchase price of your puppy is merely the first expense in the typical dog budget. Quality dog food, veterinary care (sickness and health maintenance), dog supplies and grooming costs will add up to big bucks every year. Can you adequately afford to support a canine addition to the family?

have been playing and need a rest, settling into the crate is a welcome idea. When the pups have retreated to the crate for a nap, we close the crate door and leave them quiet. You are at an advantage for crate-training if your breeder has introduced the pups to a crate.

Don't bother with a puppy-sized crate. Although your Puli will be a wee fellow when you bring him home, he will grow up in the blink of an eye and your puppy crate will be useless. Purchase a crate that will accommodate an adult Puli. A full-grown Puli can stand between 15 and 18 inches tall at the shoulder, depending on sex, so purchase a crate that will allow an adult to fully stand, lie down and turn around comfortably.

Bedding and Crate Pads

Your puppy will enjoy some type of soft bedding in his "room" (the crate), something he can snuggle into to feel cozy and secure. Old towels or blankets are good choices for a young pup, since he may (and probably will) have a toileting accident or two in the crate or decide to chew on the bedding material. Once he is fully trained and out of the early chewing stage, you can replace the puppy bedding with a permanent crate pad if you prefer. Crate pads and other dog beds run the gamut from inexpensive to high-end doggie-designer styles, but don't splurge on the good stuff until you are sure that your puppy is reliable and won't tear it up or make a mess on it.

This adorable Puli puppy is growing fast and will be adult-sized before you know it. Don't waste your money on puppy-sized food/water dishes or a puppy-sized crate.

A pup and child that grow up together form a special bond of friendship provided that interactions are supervised and both know how to behave around each other.

PUPPY TOYS

Just as infants and older children require objects to stimulate their minds and bodies, puppies need toys to entertain their curious brains, wiggly paws and achy teeth. A fun array of safe doggie toys will help satisfy your puppy's chewing instincts and distract him from gnawing on the leg of your antique chair or your new leather sofa. Most puppy toys are cute and look as if they would be a lot of fun, but not all are necessarily safe or good for your puppy, so use caution when you go puppy-toy shopping.

Puli puppies are fairly aggressive chewers. Like many other dogs, they love to chew. The best "chewcifiers" are nylon and hard rubber bones which are safe to gnaw on and come in sizes appro-priate for all age groups and breeds. Be especially careful of natural bones, which can splinter or develop dangerous sharp edges; pups can easily swallow or choke on those bone splinters. Veterinarians often tell of surgical nightmares involving bits of splintered bone, because in addition to the danger of choking, the sharp pieces can damage the intestinal tract.

Similarly, rawhide chews, while a favorite of most dogs and puppies, can be equally dangerous. Pieces of rawhide are easily swallowed after they get soft and gummy from chewing, and dogs have been known to choke on pieces of ingested rawhide. Rawhide chews should be offered only when you can supervise the puppy.

Soft woolly toys are special puppy favorites. They come in a wide variety of cute shapes and sizes; some look like little stuffed animals. Puppies love to shake them up and toss them about, or simply carry them around. Be

---

THE FIRST FAMILY MEETING
Your puppy's first day at home should be quiet and uneventful. Despite his wagging tail, he is still wondering where his mom and siblings are! Let him make friends with other members of the family on his own terms; don't overwhelm him. You have a lifetime ahead to get to know each other!

careful of fuzzy toys that have button eyes or noses that your pup could chew off and swallow, and make sure that he does not disembowel a squeaky toy to remove the squeaker! Braided rope toys are similar in that they are fun to chew and toss around, but they shred easily and the strings are easy to swallow. The strings are not digestible and, if the puppy doesn't pass them in his stool, he could end up at the vet's office. As with rawhides, your puppy should be closely monitored with rope toys.

If you believe that your pup has ingested a piece of one of his toys, check his stools for the next couple of days to see if he passes the item when he defecates. At the same time, also watch for signs of intestinal distress. A call to your veterinarian might be in order to get his advice and be on the safe side.

An all-time favorite toy for puppies (young and old!) is the empty gallon milk jug. Hard plastic juice containers—46 ounces or more—are also excellent. Such containers make lots of noise when they are batted about, and puppies go crazy with delight as they play with them. However, they don't often last very long, so be sure to remove and replace them when they get chewed up.

A word of caution about homemade toys: be careful with your choices of non-traditional

TOYS 'R SAFE

The vast array of tantalizing puppy toys is staggering. Stroll through any pet shop or pet-supply outlet and you will see that the choices can be overwhelming. However, not all dog toys are safe or sensible. Most very young puppies enjoy soft woolly toys that they can snuggle with and carry around. (You know they have outgrown them when they shred them up!) Avoid toys that have buttons, tabs or other enhancements that can be chewed off and swallowed. Soft toys that squeak are fun, but make sure your puppy does not disembowel the toy and remove (and swallow) the squeaker. Toys that rattle or make noise can excite a puppy, but they present the same danger as the squeaky kind and so require supervision. Hard rubber toys that bounce can also entertain a pup, but make sure that the toy is too big for your pup to swallow.

play objects. Never use old shoes or socks, since a puppy cannot distinguish between the old ones on which he's allowed to chew and the new ones in your closet

NEW RELEASES
Most breeders release their puppies between eight and ten weeks of age. A breeder who allows puppies to leave the litter at five or six weeks of age is likely more concerned with profit than with the puppies' welfare. However, some breeders of show or working breeds may hold one or more top-quality puppies longer in order to evaluate the puppies' career or show potential and decide which one(s) they will keep for themselves.

that are strictly off limits. That principle applies to anything that resembles something that you don't want your puppy to chew.

COLLARS
A lightweight nylon collar is the best choice for a very young pup. Quick-click collars are easy to put on and remove, and they can be adjusted as the puppy (and his coat) grows. Introduce him to his collar as soon as he comes home to get him accustomed to wearing it. He'll get used to it quickly and won't mind a bit. Make sure that it is snug enough that it won't slip off, yet loose enough to be comfortable for the pup. You should be able to slip two fingers between the collar and his neck. Check the collar often, as puppies grow in spurts, and his collar can become too tight almost overnight. Choke collars are for training purposes only but are not suitable for Pulik of any age, as this type of collar will pull and damage the coat.

LEASHES
A 6-foot nylon lead is an excellent choice for a young puppy. It is lightweight and not as tempting to chew as a leather lead. You can switch to a 6-foot leather lead after your pup has grown and is used to walking politely on a lead. For initial puppy walks and house-training purposes, you should invest in a shorter lead so

COLLARING OUR CANINES

The standard flat collar with a buckle or a snap, in leather, nylon or cotton, is widely regarded as the everyday all-purpose collar. If the collar fits correctly, you should be able to fit two fingers between the collar and the dog's neck.

Leather Buckle Collars

Limited-Slip Collar

Snap-Bolt Choke Collar

The martingale, Greyhound or limited-slip collar is preferred by many dog owners and trainers. It is fixed with an extra loop that tightens when pressure is applied to the leash. The martingale collar gets tighter but does not "choke" the dog. The limited-slip collar should only be used for walking and training, not for free play or interaction with another dog. These types of collar should never be left on the dog, as the extra loop can lead to accidents.

Choke collars, usually made of stainless steel, are made for training purposes, though are not recommended for small dogs or heavily coated breeds like the Puli. The chains can injure small dogs or damage long/abundant coats. Thin nylon choke leads are commonly used on show dogs while in the ring, though they are not practical for everyday use.

The harness, with two or three straps that attach over the dog's shoulders and around his torso, is a humane and safe alternative to the conventional collar. By and large, a well-made harness is virtually escape-proof. Harnesses are available in nylon and mesh and can be outfitted on most dogs, with chest girths ranging from 10 to 30 inches.

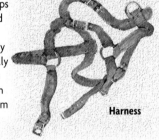

Harness

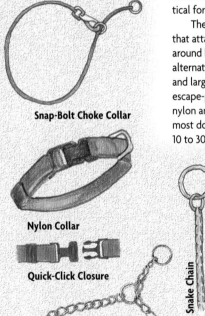

Nylon Collar

Quick-Click Closure

Snake Chain

Chrome Steel

Fur-Saver

Choke Chain Collars

A head collar, composed of a nylon strap that goes around the dog's muzzle and a second strap that wraps around his neck, offers the owner better control over his dog. This device is recommended for problem-solving with dogs (including jumping up, pulling and aggressive behaviors), but must be used with care.

A training halter, including a flat collar and two straps, made of nylon and webbing, is designed for walking. There are several on the market; some are more difficult to put on the dog than others. The halter harness, with two small slip rings at each end, is recommended for ease of use.

The Puli puppy coat is very different from that of the adult, but the coat needs proper care at all stages of life.

that you have more control over the puppy. At first you don't want him wandering too far away from you, and when taking him out for toileting you will want to keep him in the specific area chosen for his potty spot.

Once the puppy is heel-trained with a traditional leash, you can consider purchasing a retractable lead. A retractable lead is excellent for walking adult dogs that are already leash-wise. This type of lead allows the dog to roam farther away from you and explore a wider area when out walking, and also retracts when you need to keep him close to you. A safe retractable lead must be strong enough to accommodate your Puli's adult weight; check the weight limits before buying one.

HOME SAFETY FOR YOUR PUPPY

The importance of puppy-proofing cannot be overstated. In addition to making your house comfortable for your Puli's arrival, you also must make sure that your house is safe for your puppy before you bring him home. There are countless hazards in the owner's personal living environment that a pup can sniff, chew, swallow or destroy. Many are obvious; others are not. Do a thorough advance house check to remove or rearrange those things that could hurt your puppy, keeping any potentially dangerous items out of areas to which he will have access.

Electrical cords are especially dangerous, since puppies view

PUPPY PARASITES

Parasites are nasty little critters that live in or on your dog or puppy. Most puppies are born with ascarid roundworms, which are acquired from dormant ascarids residing in the dam. Other parasites can be acquired through contact with infected fecal matter. Take a stool sample to your vet for testing. He will prescribe a safe wormer to treat any parasites found in your puppy's stool. Always have a fecal test performed at your puppy's annual veterinary exam.

TOXIC PLANTS

Plants are natural puppy magnets, but many can be harmful, even fatal, if ingested by a puppy or adult dog. Scout your yard and home interior and remove any plants, bushes or flowers that could be even mildly dangerous. It could save your puppy's life. You can obtain a complete list of toxic plants from your veterinarian, at the public library or by looking online.

them as irresistible chew toys. Unplug and remove all exposed cords or fasten them beneath baseboards where the puppy cannot reach them. Veterinarians and firefighters can tell you horror stories about electrical burns and house fires that resulted from puppy-chewed electrical cords. Consider this a most serious precaution for your puppy and the rest of your family.

Scout your home for tiny objects that might be seen at a pup's eye level. Keep medication bottles and cleaning supplies well out of reach, and do the same with waste baskets and other trash containers. It goes without saying that you should not use rodent poison or other toxic chemicals in any puppy area and that you must keep such containers safely locked up. You will be amazed at how many places a curious puppy can discover!

Once your house has cleared inspection, check your yard. A sturdy fence, well embedded into the ground to prevent digging under, will give your dog a safe place to play and potty. Pulik are very athletic dogs, so a 6-foot-high fence will be required to contain an agile youngster or adult. Check the fence periodically for necessary repairs. If there is a weak link or space to squeeze through, you can be sure a determined Puli will discover it.

The garage and shed can be hazardous places for a pup, as things like fertilizers, chemicals and tools are usually kept there. It's best to keep these areas off limits to the pup. Antifreeze is especially dangerous to dogs, as they find the taste appealing and

As "on the go" as puppies are, they need plenty of time to rest, too. What better way than to relax with a friend?

it takes only a few licks from the driveway to kill a dog, puppy or adult, small breed or large.

VISITING THE VETERINARIAN

A good veterinarian is your Puli puppy's best health-insurance policy. If you do not already have a vet, ask friends and experienced dog people in your area for recommendations so that you can select a vet before you bring your Puli puppy home. Perhaps your breeder can suggest a vet in your area with experience in the breed. Also arrange for your puppy's first veterinary examination beforehand, since many vets do not have appointments immediately available and your puppy should visit the vet within a day or so of coming home.

It's important to make sure your puppy's first visit to the vet is a pleasant and positive one. The vet should take great care to befriend the pup and handle him gently to make their first meeting a positive experience. The vet will give the pup a thorough physical examination and set up a schedule for vaccinations and other necessary wellness visits. Be sure to show your vet any health and inoculation records, which you should have received from your breeder. Your vet is a great source of canine health information, so be sure to ask questions and take notes. Creating a health journal for your puppy will make a handy reference for his wellness and any future health problems that may arise.

MEETING THE FAMILY

Your Puli's homecoming is an exciting time for all members of the family, and it's only natural that everyone will be eager to meet him, pet him and play with him. However, for the puppy's sake, it's best to make these initial family meetings as uneventful as possible so that the pup is not overwhelmed with too much too soon. Remember, he has just left his dam and his littermates and is away from the breeder's home for

ASK THE VET

Help your vet help you to become a well-informed dog owner. Don't be shy about becoming involved in your puppy's veterinary care by asking questions and gaining as much knowledge as you can. For starters, ask what shots your puppy is getting and what diseases they prevent, and discuss with your vet the safest way to vaccinate. Find out what is involved in your dog's annual wellness visits. If you plan to spay or neuter, discuss the best age at which to have this done. Start out on the right "paw" with your puppy's vet and develop good communication with him, as he will care for your dog's health throughout the dog's entire life.

the first time. Despite his fuzzy wagging tail, he is still apprehensive and wondering where he is and who all these strange humans are. It's best to let him explore on his own and meet the family members as he feels comfortable. Let him investigate all the new smells, sights and sounds at his own pace. Children should be especially careful to not get overly excited, use loud voices or hug the pup too tightly. Be calm, gentle and affectionate, and be ready to comfort him if he appears frightened or uneasy.

Be sure to show your puppy his new crate during this first day home. Toss a treat or two inside the crate; if he associates the crate with food, he will associate the crate with good things. If he is comfortable with the crate, you can offer him his first meal inside it. Leave the door ajar so he can wander in and out as he chooses.

FIRST NIGHT IN HIS NEW HOME
So much has happened in your Puli puppy's first day away from the breeder. He's had his first car ride to his new home. He's met his new human family and perhaps the other family pets. He has explored his new house and yard, at least those places where he is to be allowed during his first weeks at home. He may have visited his new veterinarian. He has eaten his first meal or two

FIRST CAR RIDE
The ride to your home from the breeder may be your puppy's first automobile experience, and you should make every effort to keep him comfortable and secure. Bring a large towel or small blanket for the puppy to lie on during the trip and an extra towel in case the pup gets carsick or has a potty accident. It's best to have another person with you to hold the puppy in his lap. Most puppies will fall fast asleep from the rolling motion of the car. If the ride is lengthy, you may have to stop so that the puppy can relieve himself, so be sure to bring a leash and collar for those stops. Avoid rest areas for potty trips, since those are frequented by many dogs, who may carry parasites or disease. It's better to stop at grassy areas near gas stations or shopping centers to prevent unhealthy exposure for your pup.

away from his dam and litter-mates. Surely that's enough to tire out an eight-week-old Puli pup...or so you hope!

It's bedtime. During the day, the pup investigated his crate, which is his new den and sleeping space, so it is not entirely strange to him. Line the crate with a soft towel or blanket that he can snuggle into and gently place him into the crate for the night. Some breeders send home a piece of bedding from where the pup slept

While at the breeder's home, Puli puppies compete at mealtime. Once in your home, your puppy should learn to eat at a more leisurely pace.

with his littermates, and those familiar scents are a great comfort for the puppy on his first night without his siblings.

He will probably whine or cry. The puppy is objecting to the confinement and the fact that he is alone for the first time. This can be a stressful time for you as well as for the pup. It's important that you remain strong and don't let the puppy out of his crate to comfort him. He will fall asleep eventually. If you release him, the puppy will learn that crying means "out" and will continue that habit. You are laying the groundwork for future habits. Some breeders find that soft music can soothe a crying pup and help him get to sleep.

SOCIALIZING YOUR PUPPY

The first 20 weeks of your Puli puppy's life are the most important of his entire lifetime. A properly socialized puppy will grow

up to be a confident and stable adult who will be a pleasure to live with and a welcome addition to the neighborhood.

The importance of socialization cannot be overemphasized. Research on canine behavior has proven that puppies who are not exposed to new sights, sounds, people and animals during their first 20 weeks of life will grow up to be timid and fearful, even aggressive, and unable to flourish outside of their familiar home environment.

Socializing your puppy is not difficult and, in fact, will be a fun time for you both. Lead training goes hand in hand with socialization, so your puppy will be learning how to walk on a lead at the

THE CRITICAL SOCIALIZATION PERIOD

Canine research has shown that a puppy's 8th through 20th week is the most critical learning period of his life. This is when the puppy "learns to learn," a time when he needs positive experiences to build confidence and stability. Puppies who are not exposed to different people and situations outside the home during this period can grow up to be fearful and sometimes aggressive. This is also the best time for puppy lessons, since he has not yet acquired any bad habits that could undermine his ability to learn.

same time that he's meeting the neighborhood. Because the Puli is such a fascinating breed, everyone will enjoy meeting "the new kid on the block," and your outgoing pup should revel in the attention. Take him for short walks, to the park and to other dog-friendly places where he will encounter new people, especially children. Puppies automatically recognize children as "little people" and are drawn to play with them. Just make sure that you supervise these meetings and that the children do not get too rough or encourage him to play too hard. An overzealous pup can often nip too hard, frightening the child and in turn making the puppy overly excited. A bad experience in puppyhood can impact a dog for life, so a pup that has a negative experience with a child may grow up to be shy or even aggressive around children.

Take your puppy along on your daily errands. Puppies are natural "people magnets," and most people who see your pup will want to pet him. All of these encounters will help to mold him into a confident adult dog. Likewise, you will soon feel like a confident, responsible dog owner, rightly proud of your handsome Puli.

Be especially careful of your puppy's encounters and experiences during the eight- to ten-week-old period, which is also called the "fear period." This is a

GETTING ACQUAINTED
When visiting a litter, ask the breeder for suggestions on how best to interact with the puppies. If possible, get right into the middle of the pack and sit down with them. Observe which pups climb into your lap and which ones hang back. Toss a toy for them to chase and bring back to you. It's easy to fall in love with the puppy who picks you, but keep your future objectives in mind before you make your final decision.

serious imprinting period, and all contact during this time should be gentle and positive. A frightening or negative event could leave a permanent impression that could affect his future behavior if a similar situation arises.

Also make sure that your puppy has received his first and second rounds of vaccinations before you expose him to other dogs or bring him to places that other dogs may frequent. Avoid dog parks and other strange-dog areas until your vet assures you that your puppy is fully immunized and resistant to the diseases that can be passed between canines. Discuss safe socialization with your breeder, as some breeders recommend socializing the puppy even before he has received all of his inoculations.

LEADER OF THE PUPPY'S PACK

Like other canines, your puppy needs an authority figure, some-one he can look up to and regard as the leader of his "pack." His first pack leader was his dam, who taught him to be polite and not chew too hard on her ears or nip at her muzzle. He learned those same lessons from his litter-mates. If he played too rough, they cried in pain and stopped the game, which sent an important message to the rowdy puppy.

As puppies play together, they are also struggling to determine who will be the boss. Being pack animals, dogs need someone to be in charge. If a litter of puppies remained together beyond puppy-hood, one of the pups would emerge as the strongest one, the one who calls the shots.

Pulik get along very well with all members of the family if properly socialized (introduced). Here's a happy family with two- and four-legged "kids"!

Once your puppy leaves the pack, he will look intuitively for a new leader. If he does not recognize you as that leader, he will try to assume that position for himself. Of course, it is hard to imagine your adorable Puli puppy trying to be in charge when he is so small and seemingly helpless. You must remember that these are natural canine instincts. Do not cave in and allow your pup to get the upper "paw"!

Just as socialization is so important during these first 20 weeks, so too is your puppy's early education. He was born without any bad habits. He does not know what is good or bad behavior. If he does things like nipping and digging, it's because he is having fun and doesn't know that humans consider these things as "bad." It's your job to teach him proper puppy manners, and this is the best time to accomplish that—before he has developed bad habits, since it is much more difficult to "unlearn" or correct unacceptable learned behavior than to teach good behavior from the start.

Make sure that all members of the family understand the importance of being consistent when training their new puppy. If you tell the puppy to stay off the sofa and your daughter allows him to cuddle on the couch to watch her favorite television show, your pup will be confused about what he is and is not allowed to do. Have a family conference before your pup comes home so that everyone understands the basic principles of puppy training and the rules you have set forth for the pup, and agrees to follow them.

The old saying that "an ounce of prevention is worth a pound of cure" is especially true when it comes to puppies. It is much easier to prevent inappropriate behavior than it is to change it. It's also easier and less stressful for the pup, since it will keep discipline to a minimum and create a more positive learning environment for him. That, in turn, will also be easier on you!

Here are a few commonsense tips to keep your belongings safe and your puppy out of trouble:

- Keep your closet doors closed and your shoes, socks and other apparel off the floor so your puppy can't get at them.

A SMILE'S WORTH A MILE

Don't embark on your puppy's training course when you're not in the mood. Never train your puppy if you're feeling grouchy or impatient with him. Subjecting your puppy to your bad mood is a bad move. Your pup will sense your negative attitude, and neither of you will enjoy the session or have any measure of success. Always begin and end your training sessions on a happy note.

Dogs of most any breed that are well socialized with other dogs as pups will grow up to welcome making the acquaintance of new canine friends.

investigate their surroundings. However, you will have to teach your puppy that chewing on anything other than his toys is not acceptable. That won't happen overnight and at times puppy teeth will test your patience. However, if you allow nipping and chewing to continue, just think about the damage that a mature Puli can do with a full set of adult teeth.

Whenever your puppy nips your hand or fingers, cry out "Ouch!" in a loud voice, which should startle your puppy and stop him from nipping, even if only for a moment. Immediately distract him by offering a small treat or an appropriate toy for him to chew instead (which means having chew toys and puppy treats handy or in your pockets at all times). Praise him when he takes the toy and tell him what a good fellow he is. Praise is just as or even more important in puppy training as discipline and correction.

- Keep a secure lid on the trash container or put the trash where your puppy can't dig into it. He can't damage what he can't reach!
- Supervise your puppy at all times to make sure he is not getting into mischief. If he starts to chew the corner of the rug, you can distract him instantly by tossing a toy for him to fetch. You also will be able to whisk him outside when you notice that he is about to piddle on the carpet. If you can't see your puppy, you can't teach him or correct his behavior.

SOLVING PUPPY PROBLEMS

CHEWING AND NIPPING
Nipping at fingers and toes is normal puppy behavior. Chewing is also the way that puppies

ESTABLISH A ROUTINE
Routine is very important to a puppy's learning environment. To facilitate house-training, use the same exit/entrance door for potty trips and always take the puppy to the same place in the yard. The same principle of consistency applies to all other aspects of puppy training.

Puppies also tend to nip at children more often than adults, since they perceive little ones to be more vulnerable and more similar to their littermates. Teach your children appropriate responses to nipping behavior. If they are unable to handle it themselves, you may have to intervene. Puppy nips can be quite painful and a child's frightened reaction will only encourage a puppy to nip harder, which is a natural canine response. As with all other puppy situations, interaction between your Puli puppy and children should be supervised.

Chewing on objects, not just family members' fingers and ankles, is also normal canine behavior that can be especially tedious (for the owner, not the pup) during the teething period when the puppy's adult teeth are coming in. At this stage, chewing just plain feels good. Furniture legs and cabinet corners are common puppy favorites. Shoes and other personal items also taste pretty good to a pup.

The best solution is, once again, prevention. If you value something, keep it tucked away and out of reach. You can't hide your dining-room table in a closet, but you can try to deflect the chewing by spraying a bitter product on the objects of your dog's chewing attention. Made just to deter dogs from chewing, this substance is vile-tasting, although safe for dogs, and most puppies will avoid the forbidden object after one tiny taste. You also can apply the product to your leather leash if the puppy tries to chew on his lead during leash-training sessions.

Keep a ready supply of safe chews handy to offer your Puli as a distraction when he starts to chew on something that's a "no-no." Remember, at this tender age he does not yet know what is permitted or forbidden, so you have to be "on call" every minute he's awake and on the prowl.

You may lose a treasure or two during puppy's growing-up period, and the furniture could sustain a nasty nick or two. These

TEETHING TIME
All puppies chew. It's normal canine behavior. Chewing just plain feels good to a puppy, especially during the three- to five-month teething period when the adult teeth are breaking through the gums. Rather than attempting to eliminate such a strong natural chewing instinct, you will be more successful if you redirect it and teach your puppy what he may or may not chew. Correct inappropriate chewing with a sharp "No!" and offer him a chew toy, praising him when he takes it. Don't become discouraged. Chewing usually decreases after the adult teeth have come in.

can be trying times, so be prepared for those inevitable accidents and comfort yourself in knowing that this too shall pass.

JUMPING UP

Puli puppies are enthusiastic and outgoing, and puppies jump up—on you, your guests, your counters and your furniture. Just another normal part of growing up, and one you need to meet head-on before it becomes an ingrained habit.

The key to jump correction is consistency. You cannot correct your Puli for jumping up on you today, then allow it to happen tomorrow by greeting him with hugs and kisses. As you have learned by now, consistency is critical to all puppy lessons.

For starters, try turning your back as soon as the puppy jumps. Jumping up is a means of gaining your attention and, if the pup can't see your face, he may get discouraged and learn that he loses eye contact with his beloved master when he jumps up.

Leash corrections also work, and most puppies respond well to a leash tug if they jump. Grasp the leash close to the puppy's collar and give a quick tug downward, using the command "Off." Do not use the word "Down," since "Down" is used to teach the puppy to lie down, which is a separate action that he will learn during his education in the basic

commands. As soon as the puppy has backed off, tell him to sit and immediately praise him for doing so. This will take many repetitions and won't be accomplished quickly, so don't get discouraged or give up; you must be even more persistent than your puppy.

A second method used for jump correction is the spritzer bottle. Fill a spray bottle with water mixed with a bit of lemon juice or vinegar. As soon as the puppy jumps, command him "Off" and spritz him with the water mixture. Of course, that means having the spray bottle handy whenever or wherever jumping usually happens.

Yet a third method to discourage jumping is grasping the puppy's paws and holding them gently but firmly until he struggles to get away. Wait a brief moment or two, then release his paws and give him a command to sit. He should eventually learn that jumping gets him into an uncomfortable predicament.

Children are major victims of puppy jumping, since puppies view little people as ready targets for jumping up as well as nipping. If your children (or their friends) are unable to dispense jump corrections, you will have to intervene and handle it for them.

Important to prevention is also knowing what you should not do. Never kick your Puli (for any reason, not just for jumping) or knock him in the chest with your knee. That maneuver could actually harm your puppy. Vets can tell you stories about puppies who suffered broken bones after being banged about when they jumped up.

PUPPY WHINING

Puppies often cry and whine, just as infants and little children do. It's their way of telling us that they are lonely or in need of attention. Your puppy will miss his littermates and will feel insecure when he is left alone. You may be out of the house or just in another room, but he will still feel alone. During these times, the puppy's crate should be his personal comfort station, a place all his own where he can feel safe and secure. Once he learns that being alone is okay and not something to be feared, he will settle down without crying or objecting. You might want to leave a radio on while he is crated, as the sound of human voices can be soothing and will give the impression that people are around.

Give your puppy a favorite cuddly toy or chew toy to entertain him whenever he is crated. You will both be happier: the puppy because he is safe in his den and you because he is quiet, safe and not getting into puppy escapades that can wreak havoc in your house or cause him danger.

To make sure that your puppy will always view his crate as a safe and cozy place, never, ever use the crate as punishment. That's the best way to turn the crate into a negative place that the pup will want to avoid. Sure, you can use the crate for your own peace of mind if your puppy is getting into trouble and needs some "time out." Just don't let him know that. Never scold the pup and immediately place him into the crate. Count to ten, give him a couple of hugs and maybe a treat, then scoot him into his crate.

It's also important not to make a big fuss when he is released from the crate. That will make getting out of the crate more appealing than being in the crate, which is just the opposite of what you are trying to achieve.

Everything looks tempting to a teething pup—and puppy teeth can certainly inflict pain! Discourage nipping early on and be consistent in telling your mouthy puppy "No!"

PROPER CARE OF YOUR

PULI

Adding a Puli to your household means adding a new family member who will need your care each and every day. When your Puli pup first comes home, you will start a routine with him so that, as he grows up, your dog will have a daily schedule just as you do. The aspects of your dog's daily care will likewise become regular parts of your day, so you'll both have a new schedule. Dogs learn by consistency and thrive on routine: regular times for meals, exercise, grooming and potty trips are just as important for your dog as they are for you. Your dog's schedule will depend much on your family's daily routine, but remember that you now have a new member of the family who is part of your day every day.

FEEDING

Feeding a dog the best diet is based on various factors, including age, activity level, overall condition and size of breed. When you visit the breeder, he will share with you his advice about the proper diet for your dog based on his experience with the breed and the foods with which he has had success. Likewise, your vet will be a helpful source of advice throughout the dog's life and will aid you in planning a diet for optimal health.

FEEDING THE PUPPY

Of course, your pup's very first food will be his dam's milk. There may be special situations in which pups fail to nurse, necessitating that the breeder hand-feed them with a formula, but for the most part pups spend the first weeks of life nursing from their dam. The breeder weans the pups by gradually introducing solid foods and decreasing the milk meals. Pups may even start themselves off on the weaning process,

---

FEEDING IN HOT WEATHER

Even the most dedicated chow hound may have less of an appetite when the weather is hot or humid. If your dog leaves more of his food behind than usual, adjust his portions until the weather and his appetite return to normal. Never leave the uneaten portion in the bowl, hoping he will return to finish it, because higher temperatures encourage food spoilage and bacterial growth.

albeit inadvertently, if they snatch bites from their mom's food bowl.

By the time the pups are ready for new homes, they are fully weaned and eating a good puppy food. As a new owner, you may be thinking, "Great! The breeder has taken care of the hard part." Not so fast.

A puppy's first year of life is the time when all or most of his growth and development takes place. This is a delicate time, and diet plays a huge role in proper skeletal and muscular formation. Improper diet and exercise habits can lead to damaging problems that will compromise the dog's health and movement for his entire life. That being said, new owners should not worry needlessly. With the myriad types of food formulated specifically for growing pups of different-sized breeds, dog-food manufacturers have taken much of the guesswork out of feeding your puppy well. Since growth-food formulas are designed to provide the nutrition that a growing puppy needs, it is unnecessary and, in fact, can prove harmful to add supplements to the diet. Research has shown that too much of certain vitamin supplements and minerals predispose a dog to skeletal problems. It's by no means a case of "if a little is good, a lot is better." At every stage of your dog's life, too much or too little in the way of nutrients can be harmful,

which is why a manufactured complete food is the easiest way to know that your dog is getting what he needs.

Because of a young pup's small body and accordingly small

VARIETY IS THE SPICE
Although dog-food manufacturers contend that dogs don't like variety in their diets, studies show quite the opposite to be true. Dogs would much rather vary their meals than eat the same old chow day in and day out. Dry kibble is no more exciting for a dog than the same bowl of bran flakes would be for you. Fortunately, there are dozens of varieties available on the market, and your dog will likely show preference for certain flavors over others. A word of warning: don't overdo it or you'll develop a fussy eater who only prefers chopped beef fillet and asparagus tips every night.

SWITCHING FOODS

There are certain times in a dog's life when it becomes necessary to switch his food; for example, from puppy to adult food and then from adult to senior-dog food. Additionally, you may decide to feed your pup a different type of food from what he received from the breeder, and there may be "emergency" situations in which you can't find your dog's normal brand and have to offer something else temporarily. Anytime a change is made, for whatever reason, the switch must be done gradually. You don't want to upset the dog's stomach or end up with a picky eater who refuses to eat something new. A tried-and-true approach is, over the course of about a week, to mix a little of the new food in with the old, increasing the proportion of new to old as the days progress. At the end of the week, you'll be feeding his regular portions of the new food, and he will barely notice the change.

digestive system, his daily portion will be divided up into small meals throughout the day. This can mean starting off with three or more meals a day and decreasing the number of meals as the pup matures. For the adult, dividing the day's food into two meals on a morning/evening schedule is much healthier for the dog's digestion than feeding one large daily portion.

Regarding the feeding schedule, feeding the pup at the same times and in the same place each day is important for both house-breaking purposes and establishing the dog's everyday routine. As for the amount to feed, growing puppies generally need proportionately more food per body weight than their adult counterparts, but a pup should never be allowed to gain excess weight. Dogs of all ages should be kept in proper body condition, but extra weight can strain a pup's developing frame, causing skeletal problems.

Watch your pup's weight as he grows and, if the recommended amounts seem to be too much or too little for your pup, consult the vet about appropriate dietary changes. Keep in mind that treats, although small, can quickly add up throughout the day, contributing unnecessary calories. Treats are fine when used prudently; opt for dog treats specially formulated to be healthy or for nutritious snacks like small pieces of cheese or cooked chicken.

FEEDING THE ADULT DOG
For the adult (meaning physically mature) dog, feeding properly is about maintenance, not growth. Again, correct weight is a concern. Your dog should appear fit and should have an evident "waist." His ribs should not be protruding (a sign of being underweight), but they should be

covered by only a slight layer of fat. Under normal circumstances, an adult dog can be maintained fairly easily with a high-quality nutritionally complete adult-formula food.

Factor treats into your dog's overall daily caloric intake, and avoid offering table scraps. Not only are some "people foods," like chocolate, nuts, raisins, grapes, onions and large amounts of garlic, toxic to dogs but feeding from your plate encourages begging and overeating. Over-weight dogs are more prone to health problems. Research has even shown that obesity takes years off a dog's life. With that in

This Puli pack shows the true meaning of family-style dining.

mind, resist the urge to overfeed and over-treat. Don't make unnecessary additions to your dog's diet, whether with tidbits or with extra vitamins and minerals.

The amount of food needed for proper maintenance will vary depending on the individual dog's activity level, but you will be able to tell whether the daily portions are keeping him in good shape. With the wide variety of good complete foods available, choosing what to feed is largely a matter of personal preference. Just as with the puppy, the adult dog should have consistency in his mealtimes and feeding place. In addition to a consistent routine, regular mealtimes also allow the owner to see how much his dog is eating. If the dog seems never to be satisfied or, likewise, becomes uninterested in his food, the owner will know right away that something is wrong and can consult the vet. A schedule allows you also to allow the dog

NOT HUNGRY?

No dog in his right mind would turn down his dinner, would he? If you notice that your dog has lost interest in his food, there could be any number of causes. Dental problems are a common cause of appetite loss, one that is often overlooked. If your dog has a toothache, a loose tooth or sore gums from infection, chances are it doesn't feel so good to chew. Think about when you've had a toothache! If your dog does not approach the food bowl with his usual enthusiasm, look inside his mouth for signs of a problem. Whatever the cause, you'll want to consult your vet so that your chow hound can get back to his happy, hungry self as soon as possible.

adequate rest before and after eating, as no dog should exercise too close to mealtimes.

DIETS FOR THE AGING DOG
A good rule of thumb is that once a dog has reached around 75% of his expected lifespan, he has reached "senior citizen" or

DIET DON'TS
- Got milk? Don't give it to your dog! Dogs cannot tolerate large quantities of cows' milk, as they do not have the enzymes to digest lactose.
- You may have heard of dog owners who add raw eggs to their dogs' food for a shiny coat or to make the food more palatable, but consumption of raw eggs too often can cause a deficiency of the vitamin biotin.
- Avoid feeding table scraps, as they will upset the balance of the dog's complete food. Additionally, fatty or highly seasoned foods can cause upset canine stomachs.
- Do not offer raw meat to your dog. Raw meat can contain parasites; it also is high in fat.
- Vitamin A toxicity in dogs can be caused by too much raw liver, especially if the dog already gets enough vitamin A in his balanced diet, which should be the case.
- Bones like chicken, pork chop and other soft bones are not suitable, as they easily splinter.

geriatric status. Your Puli will be considered a senior at about 7 or 8 years of age; he has a projected lifespan of about 10–15 years, with many reaching their mid-teens in this hardy and robust breed.

What does aging have to do with your dog's diet? No, he won't get a discount at the local diner's early-bird special. Yes, he will require some dietary changes to accommodate the changes that come along with increased age. One change is that the older dog's dietary needs become more similar to that of a puppy. Specifically, dogs can metabolize more protein as youngsters and seniors than in the adult-maintenance stage. Discuss with your vet whether you need to switch to a higher-protein or senior-formulated food or whether your current adult-dog food contains sufficient nutrition for the senior.

Watching the dog's weight remains essential, even more so in the senior stage. Older dogs are already more vulnerable to illness, and obesity only contributes to their susceptibility to problems. As the older dog becomes less active and thus exercises less, his regular portions may cause him to gain weight. At this point, you may consider decreasing his daily food intake or switching to a reduced-calorie food. As with other changes, you should consult your vet for advice.

DON'T FORGET THE WATER!

For a dog, it's always time for a drink! Regardless of what type of food he eats, there's no doubt that he needs plenty of water. Fresh cold water, in a clean bowl, should be available to your dog indoors and outdoors. There are special circumstances, such as during puppy housebreaking, when you will want to monitor your pup's water intake so that you will be able to predict when he will need to relieve himself, but water must be available to him nonetheless. Water is essential for hydration and proper body function just as it is in humans.

You will get to know how much your dog typically drinks in a day. Of course, in the heat or if exercising vigorously, he will be more thirsty and will drink more. However, if he begins to drink noticeably more water for no apparent reason, this could signal any of various problems, and you are advised to consult your vet.

Water is the best drink for dogs. Some owners are tempted to give milk from time to time or to moisten dry food with milk, but dogs do not have the enzymes necessary to digest the lactose in milk, which is much different from the milk that nursing puppies receive. Therefore, stick with clean fresh water to quench your dog's thirst, and always have it readily available to him.

EXERCISE

We all know the importance of exercise for humans, so it should come as no surprise that it is essential for our canine friends as

QUENCHING HIS THIRST

Is your dog drinking more than normal and trying to lap up everything in sight? Excessive drinking has many different causes. Obvious causes for a dog's being thirstier than usual are hot weather and vigorous exercise. However, if your dog is drinking more for no apparent reason, you could have cause for concern. Serious conditions like kidney or liver disease, diabetes and various types of hormonal problems can all be indicated by excessive drinking. If you notice your dog's being excessively thirsty, contact your vet at once. Hopefully there will be a simpler explanation, but the earlier a serious problem is detected, the sooner it can be treated, with a better rate of cure.

A LITTLE GOES A LONG WAY
When the course of inoculations is complete, then you will be able to take the puppy into public places. Until then, you will have to be content with little games in the yard and the start of those first collar-and-lead training sessions. Food is converted into energy and growth. If you allow excessive exercise, then growth will surely suffer. A guide in those early days is that nothing should be done in excess. Food, play, a little walk and lots of sleep are the priorities.

well. Now, regardless of your own level of fitness, get ready to assume the role of personal trainer for your dog. It's not as hard as it sounds, and it will have health benefits for you, too.

Just as with anything else you do with your dog, you must set a routine for his exercise. It's the same as your daily morning run before work or never missing the 7 p.m. aerobics class. If you plan it and get into the habit of actually doing it, it will become just another part of your day. Think of it as making daily exercise appointments with your dog, and stick to your schedule.

As a rule, Pulik in normal health should have about an hour of activity each day. Dogs with health or orthopedic problems may have specific limitations, so their exercise plans are best

devised with the help of a vet. For healthy dogs, there are many ways to fit the required activity into your day. Depending on your schedule, you may plan a walk or activity session in the morning and again in the evening, or do it all at once in a long session each day. Walking is the most popular way to exercise a dog (it's good for you, too!); other suggestions include retrieving games, jogging and disc-catching or other active games with his toys. A Puli will delight in free-running time in a safely enclosed area. Not all Pulik are good swimmers, so a Puli in water must *always* be closely supervised even if he shows swimming ability.

On that note, some precautions should be taken with a puppy's exercise. During his first year, when he is growing and developing, your Puli should not be subject to stressful activity that stresses his body. Short walks at a comfortable pace and play sessions in the fenced yard are good for a growing pup, and his exercise can be increased as he grows up.

For overweight dogs, dietary changes and activity will help the goal of weight loss. (Sound familiar?) While they should of course be encouraged to be active, remember not to overdo it, as the excess weight is already putting strain on their vital organs and bones. As for highly active dogs, some of them never seem to tire! They will enjoy time spent with their owners doing things together.

Regardless of your dog's condition and activity level, exercise offers benefits to all dogs and owners. Consider the fact that dogs who are kept active are more stimulated both physically and mentally, meaning that they are less likely to become bored and lapse into destructive behavior. Also consider the benefits of one-on-one time with your dog every day, continually strengthening the bond between the two of you. Furthermore, exercising together will improve health and longevity for both of you. You both need exercise, and now you and your dog have a workout partner and motivator!

GROOMING

One major consideration when rearing this breed is the coat. The Puli is born with a fairly closely laid jacket that soon starts to grow and stand away from the body. Early grooming begins with brushing the hair in the direction from the tail toward the head. The hair grows longer and then it will start to make attempts to go into little "rat tails." It is at this stage that Mother Nature decides the formation of the future coat, and you should not try to alter it in any way. Some hairs will start to split into quite fine strands while others may be distinctly thicker.

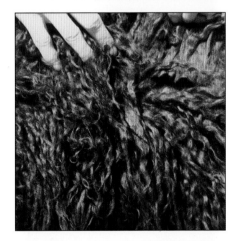

From top to bottom, these pictures show the progression of three stages of cord development in the Puli's coat. The bottom picture shows an adult coat.

Yes, the Puli does have eyes underneath all of those cords!

Trimming the hair around the anal pore is necessary for health and hygiene reasons, as well as comfort to the dog.

As soon as the coat indicates it is about to start cording, all brushing and combing stops. To encourage the formation and firming up of the baby cords, a light spray each day with soft water can be helpful. As the embryo cords lengthen, they will normally start to thicken a little, and it is at this stage that you must devote time to working your way through the whole coat, ensuring that the forming cords are separated right down to the skin. It is most important that any light fluff between the cords is plucked out, so that air can reach the skin. If the hairs at skin level are allowed to remain, they will thicken and will not only prevent air from getting in but also cause irritation to the skin. Indeed, in extreme cases, these hairs can become host to some little undesirable passen-gers, i.e., parasites. The loose fluffy hair, if removed without delay, allows the forming cords to remain separated. The actual separation into cords can start at any time from around six months of age, and it may be almost a year before the cords are firm and separate.

Do check certain areas where there is a greater risk of felting up. Under the ear flaps, under the lower jaw, around the throat, behind the elbows and inside the hindlegs are the likely places. Check also on top of the body, where the coat comes under the tail.

The formation of the cords is a natural progression, yet still needs attention. The forming cords should be kept separate, ensuring that air can reach the skin and that any loose fluffy hairs are removed.

Varying types of cords can be found within a single litter, and it is advised that you should not try to alter their size or shape. If you attempt to thin down a thicker cord, you will contribute to the cord's weakening, and in time these weaker cords can become worn and fall off. The consistency of good cords can be likened to a woolly garment that has started to felt up. The more you wash and rub it, the firmer the mats become—that is what happens with a corded coat. Once firm and properly corded, these strands don't come undone. A well-tended corded coat will always attract attention and admiration,

and the hours spent on it in the early days will be a worthwhile investment.

A common misunderstanding of the inexperienced owner is the belief that when you put the Puli in water, all cords become undone, and then you have to knit or plait them up after every bath. Of course this is nonsense—thank heavens!

There are many types of shampoos and conditioners available. We use an insecticidal shampoo followed by a good-quality lanolin conditioner to prevent the cords' drying out and becoming discolored. Dead hair tends to turn brown or chestnut red, and

When our dogs are bathed, we check that anal glands are clear. The anal glands are situated on each side of the anal pore and produce a liquid that helps lubricate the dog's motions. If there is no firmness to the excreta, then the glands don't lubricate, so they may start to build up a foul-smelling fluid accumulation. If left, the glands can become impacted, which in extreme cases can turn into an abscess, causing soreness

Part of the grooming process includes cleaning your Puli's ears and checking for ear mites, odor and/or other signs of a problem.

the ends of the cords, being composed of the oldest hair, will often turn brown, especially on black or gray dogs.

New owners frequently ask many questions about the Puli's coat, including whether or not Pulik shed. The answer is, not quite as much as other dogs do, but shedding is responsible for the formation of the Puli's cords. The cords are formed by the longer harsher hair's twisting and trapping the discarded undercoat. Other questions are whether Pulik get too hot under all their cords and if they can feel the cold. They can get rather warm, but the coat provides natural insulation, serving to keep the strong sunshine off the body to avoid burning and to retain the body warmth, preventing wind and rain from reaching the underparts.

SCOOTING HIS BOTTOM

Here's a doggy problem that many owners tend to neglect. If your dog is scooting his rear end around the carpet, he probably is experiencing anal-sac impaction or blockage. The anal sacs are the two grape-sized glands on either side of the dog's vent. The dog cannot empty these glands, which become filled with a foul-smelling material. The dog may attempt to lick the area to relieve the pressure. He may also rub his anus on your walls, furniture or floors.

Don't neglect your dog's rear end during grooming sessions. By squeezing both sides of the anus with a soft cloth, you can express some of the material in the sacs. If the material is pasty and thick, you likely will need the assistance of a veterinarian. Vets know how to express the glands and can show you how to do it correctly without hurting the dog or spraying yourself with the unpleasant liquid.

PRESERVING THOSE PEARLY WHITES

What do you treasure more than the smile of your beloved canine pal? Brushing your dog's teeth is just as important as brushing your own. Neglecting your dog's teeth can lead to tooth loss, periodontal disease and inflamed gums, not to mention bad breath. Can you find the time to brush your dog's teeth every day? If not, you should do so once a week at the very least, though every day is truly the ideal. Your vet should give your dog a thorough dental examination during his annual check-ups.

Pet shops sell terrific tooth-care devices, including specially designed toothbrushes, yummy toothpastes and finger-model brushes. You can use a human toothbrush with soft bristles, but never use human toothpastes, which can damage the dog's enamel. Baking soda is an alternative to doggie toothpastes, but your dog will be more receptive to canine toothpastes with the flavor of liver or hamburger. Make tooth care fun for your dog. Let him think that you're "horsing around" with his mouth. When brushing the dog's teeth, begin with the largest teeth (the canines) and proceed back toward the molars.

and pain. Your vet will show you how to check and express these glands so that with regular inspection at bath time, you should never have problems. While on the subject, we always check the hair surrounding the anus, keeping it well trimmed so that it does not become matted or clogged.

EAR CLEANING

While keeping your dog's ears clean unfortunately will not cause him to "hear" your commands any better, it will protect him from ear infection and ear-mite infestation. In addition, a dog's ears are vulnerable to waxy build-up and to collecting foreign matter from the outdoors. Look in your dog's ears regularly to ensure that they look pink, clean and otherwise healthy. Even if they look fine, an odor in the ears signals a problem and means it's time to call the vet.

A dog's ears should be cleaned regularly; once a week is suggested. Using a cotton ball or pad, and never probing into the ear canal, wipe the ear gently. You

Strong white teeth are important not just for a sparkling smile but also for your Puli's internal health. Don't neglect his home dental care.

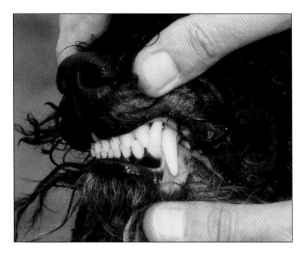

can use an ear-cleansing liquid or powder available from your vet or pet-supply store; alternatively, you might prefer to use home-made solutions with ingredients like one part white vinegar and one part hydrogen peroxide. Ask your vet about home remedies before you attempt to concoct something on your own!

Keep your dog's ears free of excess hair by plucking it as needed. If done gently, this will be painless for the dog. Look for wax, brown droppings (a sign of ear mites), redness or any other abnormalities. At the first sign of a problem, contact your vet so that he can prescribe an appropriate medication.

NAIL CLIPPING

Having their nails trimmed is not on many dogs' lists of favorite things to do. With this in mind, you will need to accustom your puppy to the procedure at a young age so that he will sit still (well, as still as he can) for his pedi-cures. Long nails can cause the dog's feet to spread, which is not good for him; likewise, long nails can hurt if they unintentionally scratch, not good for you.

A dog who walks frequently on hard surfaces like cement may require less frequent nail clipping; check the length regularly and clip as needed.

THE MONTHLY GRIND

If your dog doesn't like the feeling of nail clippers or if you're not comfortable using them, you may wish to try an electric nail grinder. This tool has a small sandpaper disc on the end that rotates to grind the nails down. Some feel that using a grinder reduces the risk of cutting into the quick; this can be true if the tool is used properly. Usually you will be able to tell where the quick is before you get to it. A benefit of the grinder is that it creates a smooth finish on the nails so that there are no ragged edges. Because the tool makes noise, your dog should be introduced to it before the actual grinding takes place. Turn it on and let your dog hear the noise; turn it off and let him inspect it with you holding it. Use the grinder gently, holding it firmly and progressing a little at a time until you reach the proper length. Look at the nail as you grind so that you do not go too short. Stop at any indication that you are nearing the quick. It will take a few sessions for both you and the puppy to get used to the grinder. Make sure that you don't let his hair get tangled in the grinder!

Some dogs' nails are worn down naturally by regular walking on hard surfaces, so the frequency with which you clip depends on your individual dog. Look at his nails from time to time and clip as needed; a good way to know when it's time for a trim is if you hear your dog clicking as he walks across the floor.

There are several types of nail clippers and even electric nail-grinding tools made for dogs; first we'll discuss using the clipper. To start, have your clipper ready and some doggie treats on hand. You want your pup to view his nail-clipping sessions in a positive light, and what better way to convince him than with food? You may want to enlist the help of an assistant to comfort the pup and offer treats as you concentrate on the clipping itself. The guillotine-type clipper is thought of by many as the easiest type to use; the nail tip is inserted into the opening, and blades on the top and bottom snip it off in one clip.

Start by grasping the pup's paw; a little pressure on the foot pad causes the nail to extend, making it easier to clip. Clip off a little at a time. If you can see the "quick," which is a blood vessel that runs through each nail, you will know how much to trim, as you do not want to cut into the quick. On that note, if you do cut the quick, which will cause bleeding, you can stem the flow of

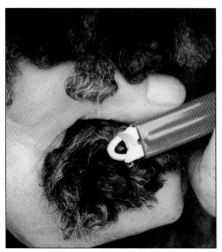

You can purchase special nail clippers made for use on dogs. The guillotine type, shown here, is easy to use, as it removes the nail tip in one quick motion.

blood with a styptic pencil or other clotting agent. If you mistakenly nip the quick, do not panic or fuss, as this will cause the pup to be afraid. Simply reassure the pup, stop the bleeding and move on to the next nail. Don't be discouraged; you will become a professional canine pedicurist with practice.

You may or may not be able to see the quick, so it's best to just clip off a small bit at a time. If you see a dark dot in the center of the nail, this is the quick and your cue to stop clipping. Tell the puppy he's a "good boy" and offer a piece of treat with each nail. You can also use nail-clipping time to examine the footpads, making sure that they are not dry and cracked and that nothing has become embedded in them.

The nail grinder, the other choice, is many owners' first

IF YOU FIND A LOST DOG

If you find a lost dog and want to help, here are some tips. First of all, the dog may act unpredictably, so assess the situation. If you feel uneasy, don't try to approach him. Instead, call the local police department or humane society. If the dog looks friendly and has a collar with an ID tag, approach him carefully. Squat down and extend a hand so that he can sniff it. Be gentle and speak in a friendly tone. Hopefully he will come near enough so that you can get the information from his tags. If he has no identification, and you can transport the dog, you can take him to a humane society or to your own home, though you should advise the local authorities and animal shelters that you have found a dog, as most owners will contact these agencies first if their dog is missing. If you take the dog to a shelter or humane society, be sure to find out the agency's policies before leaving him there. Many town and county shelters are crowded and only have a limited holding period.

If you find a badly injured animal with no identification, you have several things to think about. Taking him to an animal shelter does not necessarily mean that he will be all fixed up and ready to adopt. If you choose to take the dog to a private vet, you must be ready to assume the costs of his treatment.

It's natural to want to rescue a stray or lost dog, so do what you can. After all, if your own dog ended up in the same situation, wouldn't you hope that someone else would take the time to help him?

choice. Accustoming the puppy to the sound of the grinder and sensation of the buzz presents fewer challenges than the clipper, and there's no chance of cutting through the quick. Use the grinder on a low setting and always talk soothingly to your dog. He won't mind his salon visit, and he'll have nicely polished nails as well.

IDENTIFICATION FOR YOUR DOG

You love your Puli and want to keep him safe. Of course you take every precaution to prevent his escaping from the yard or becoming lost or stolen. You have a sturdy high fence and you always keep your dog on lead when out and about in public places. If your dog is not properly identified, however, you are overlooking a major aspect of his safety. We hope to never be in a situation where our dog is missing, but we should practice prevention in the unfortunate case that this happens; identification greatly increases the chances of your dog's being returned to you.

There are several ways to identify your dog. First, the traditional dog tag should be a staple in your dog's wardrobe, attached to his everyday collar. Tags can be

made of sturdy plastic and various metals and should include your contact information so that a person who finds the dog can get in touch with you right away to arrange his return. Many people today enjoy the wide range of decorative tags available, so have fun and create a tag to match your dog's personality. Of course, it is important that the tag stays on the collar, so have a secure "O" ring attachment; you also can explore the type of tag that slides right onto the collar.

In addition to the ID tag, which every dog should wear even if identified by another method, two other forms of identification have become popular: microchipping and tattooing. In microchipping, a tiny scannable chip is painlessly inserted under the dog's skin. The number is registered to you so that, if your lost dog turns up at a clinic or shelter, the chip can be scanned to retrieve your contact information.

The advantage of the microchip is that it is a permanent form of ID, but there are some factors to consider. Several different companies make microchips, and not all are compatible with the others' scanning devices. It's best to find a company with a universal microchip that can be read by scanners made by other companies as well. It won't do any good to have the dog chipped if the information cannot be retrieved. Also, not every humane society, shelter and clinic is equipped with a scanner, although more and more facilities are equipping themselves. In fact,

For safe travels, a dog should never be allowed to roam loose in a vehicle. A crate or a partition for the vehicle are two safety options.

> **CAR CAUTION**
> You may like to bring your canine companion along on the daily errands, but if you will be running in and out from place to place and can't bring him indoors with you, leave him at home. Your dog should never be left alone in the car, not even for a minute—never! A car heats up very quickly, and even a cracked-open window will not help. In fact, leaving the window cracked will be dangerous if the dog becomes uncomfortable and tries to escape. A dog alone in a car may also attract dog thieves. When in doubt, leave your dog home, where you know he will be safe.

A collar with a securely fastened ID tag is a must-wear for every dog. Even if the tag becomes detached, the collar signifies that the dog is someone's pet and makes him more likely to get help if lost.

many shelters microchip dogs that they adopt out to new homes.

In the US, there are five or six major microchip manufacturers as well as a few databases. The American Kennel Club's Companion Animal Recovery unit works in conjunction with HomeAgain™ Companion Animal Retrieval System (Schering-Plough).

Because the microchip is not visible to the eye, the dog must wear a tag that states that he is microchipped so that whoever picks him up will know to have him scanned. These tags usually also list a phone number for the microchip registry in case the chip cannot be read. He of course also must have a tag with your contact information. Humane societies and veterinary clinics offer microchipping service, which is usually very affordable.

Though less popular than microchipping, tattooing is another permanent method of ID for dogs. Most vets perform this service, and there are also clinics that perform dog tattooing. This is also an affordable procedure and one that will not cause much discomfort for the dog. It is best to put the tattoo in a visible area, such as the ear, to deter theft. It is sad to say that there are cases of dogs' being stolen and sold to research laboratories, but such laboratories will not accept tattooed dogs.

To ensure that the tattoo is effective in aiding your dog's return to you, the tattoo number must be registered with a national organization. That way, when someone finds a tattooed dog, a phone call to the registry will quickly match the dog with his owner.

DOGGONE!

Wendy Ballard is the editor and publisher of the *DogGone*™ newsletter, which comes out bi-monthly and features fun articles by dog owners who love to travel with their dogs. The newsletter includes information about fun places to go with your dogs, including popular vacation spots, dog-friendly hotels, parks, campgrounds, resorts, etc., as well as interesting activities to do with your dog, such as flyball, agility and much more. You can subscribe to the publication by contacting the publisher at PO Box 651155, Vero Beach, FL 32965-1155.

PULI

BASIC TRAINING PRINCIPLES: PUPPY VS. ADULT

There's a big difference between training an adult dog and training a young puppy. With a young puppy, everything is new! At eight to ten weeks of age, he will be experiencing many things, and he has nothing with which to compare these experiences. Up to this point, he has been with his dam and littermates, not one-on-one with people except in his interactions with his breeder and visitors to the litter.

Show dogs must be trained to accept hands-on examination, as this is how the judge evaluates a dog's structure in the ring.

SMILE WHEN YOU ORDER ME AROUND!

While trainers recommend practicing with your dog every day, it's perfectly acceptable to take a "mental health day" off. It's better not to train the dog on days when you're in a sour mood. Your bad attitude or lack of interest will be sensed by your dog, and he will respond accordingly. Studies show that dogs are well tuned in to their humans' emotions. Be conscious of how you use your voice when talking to your dog. Raising your voice or shouting will only erode your dog's trust in you as his trainer and master.

When you first bring the puppy home, he is eager to please you. This means that he accepts doing things your way. During the next couple of months, he will absorb the basis of everything he needs to know for the rest of his life. This early age is even referred to as the "sponge" stage. After that, for the next 18 months, it's up to you to reinforce good manners by building on the foundation that you've established. Once your puppy is reliable in basic commands and behavior and has reached the appropriate age, you may gradually introduce him to some of the interesting sports, games and activities available to pet owners and their dogs.

Raising your puppy is a family affair. Each member of the family must know what rules to set forth for the puppy and how to use the same one-word commands to mean exactly the same thing every time. Even if yours is a large family, one person will soon be considered by the pup to be the leader, the alpha person in his pack, the "boss" who must be obeyed. Often that highly regarded person turns out to be the one who feeds the puppy.

You mold your pup's behavior from the first day you bring him home. His natural curiosity can get him into trouble; you must set the rules for both his safety and your sanity.

> ## BASIC PRINCIPLES OF DOG TRAINING
> 1. Start training early. A young puppy is ready, willing and able.
> 2. Timing is your all-important tool. Praise at the exact time that the dog responds correctly. Pay close attention.
> 3. Patience is almost as important as timing!
> 4. Repeat! The same word has to mean the same thing every time.
> 5. In the beginning, praise all correct behavior verbally, along with treats and petting.

Food ranks very high on the puppy's list of important things. That's why your puppy is rewarded with small treats along with verbal praise when he responds to you correctly. As the puppy learns to do what you want him to do, the food rewards are gradually eliminated and only the praise remains. If you were to keep up with the food treats, you could have two problems on your hands—an obese dog and a beggar.

Training begins the minute your Puli puppy steps through the doorway of your home, so don't make the mistake of putting the puppy on the floor and telling him by your actions to "Go for it! Run wild!" Even if this is your first puppy, you must act as if you know what you're doing: be the boss. An uncertain pup may be

terrified to move, while a bold one will be ready to take you at your word and start plotting to destroy the house! Before you collected your puppy, you decided where his own special place would be, and that's where to put him when you first arrive home. Give him a house tour after he has investigated his area and had a nap and a bathroom "pit stop."

It's worth mentioning here that if you've adopted an adult dog that is completely trained to your liking, lucky you! You're off the hook! However, if that dog spent his life up to this point in a kennel, or even in a good home but without any real training, be prepared to tackle the job ahead. A dog three years of age or older with no previous training cannot be blamed for not knowing what he was never taught. While the dog is trying to understand and learn your rules, at the same time he has to unlearn many of his previously self-taught habits and general view of the world.

Working with a professional trainer will speed up your progress with an adopted adult dog. You'll need patience, too. Some new rules may be close to impossible for the dog to accept. After all, he's been successful so far by doing everything his way! (Patience again.) He may agree with your instruction for a few days and then slip back into his old ways, so you must be just as

OUR CANINE KIDS

"Everything I learned about parenting, I learned from my dog." How often adults recognize that their parenting skills are mere extensions of the education they acquired while caring for their dogs. Many owners refer to their dogs as their "kids" and treat their canine companions like real members of the family. Surveys indicate that a majority of dog owners talk to their dogs regularly, celebrate their dogs' birthdays and purchase Christmas gifts for their dogs. Another survey shows that dog owners take their dogs to the veterinarian more frequently than they visit their own physicians.

consistent and understanding in your teaching as you would be with a puppy. (More patience needed yet again!) Your dog has to

BE UPSTANDING!

You are the dog's leader. During training, stand up straight so your dog looks up at you, and therefore up *to* you. Say the command words distinctly, in a clear, declarative tone of voice. (No barking!) Give rewards only as the correct response takes place (remember your timing!). Praise, smiles and treats are "rewards" used to positively reinforce correct responses. Don't repeat a mistake. Just change to another exercise—you will soon find success!

learn to pay attention to your voice, your family, the daily routine, new smells, new sounds and, in some cases, even a new climate.

One of the most important things to find out about a newly adopted adult dog is his reaction to children (yours and others), strangers and your friends, and how he acts upon meeting other dogs. If he was not socialized with dogs as a puppy, this could be a major problem. This does not mean that he's a "bad" dog, a vicious dog or an aggressive dog; rather, it means that he has no idea how to read another dog's body language. There's no way for him to tell whether the other dog is a friend or foe. Survival instinct takes over, telling him to attack first and ask questions later. This definitely calls for professional help and, even then, may not be a behavior that can be corrected 100% reliably (or even at all). If you have a puppy, this is why it is so very important to introduce your young puppy properly to other puppies and "dog-friendly" adult dogs.

HOUSE-TRAINING YOUR PULI

Dogs are tactility-oriented when it comes to house-training. In other words, they respond to the surface on which they are given approval to eliminate. The choice is yours (the dog's version is in parentheses): The lawn (including the neighbors' lawns)? A bare patch of earth under a tree (where people like to sit and relax in the summertime)? Concrete steps or patio (all sidewalks, garages and basement floors)? The curbside (watch out for cars)? A small area of crushed stone in a corner of the yard (mine!)? The latter is the best choice if you can manage it, because it will remain strictly for the dog's use and is easy to keep clean.

You can start out with paper-training indoors and switch over to an outdoor surface as the puppy matures and gains control over his need to eliminate. For the naysayers, don't worry—this won't mean that the dog will soil

WHO'S TRAINING WHOM?

Dog training is a black-and-white exercise. The correct response to a command must be absolute, and the trainer must insist on completely accurate responses from the dog. A trainer cannot command his dog to sit and then settle for the dog's melting into the down position. Often owners are so pleased that their dogs "did something" in response to a command that they just shrug and say, "OK, down" even though they wanted the dog to sit. You want your dog to respond to the command without hesitation: he must respond at that moment and correctly every time.

on every piece of newspaper lying around the house. You are training him to go outside, remember? Starting out by paper-training often is the only choice for a city dog.

WHEN YOUR PUPPY'S "GOT TO GO"
Your puppy's need to relieve himself is seemingly non-stop, but signs of improvement will be seen each week. From 8 to 10 weeks old, the puppy will have to be taken outside every time he wakes up, about 10–15 minutes after every meal and after every period of play—all day long, from first thing in the morning until his bedtime. That's a total of ten or more trips per day to teach the puppy where it's okay to relieve

Keep your yard a clean place to play for all family members by training your dog to one specific toilet area and always cleaning up after him.

to come over to take the pup outside, feed him his lunch and then take him out again about ten or so minutes after he's eaten. Also make arrangements with that or another person to be your "emergency" contact if you have to stay late on the job. Remind yourself—repeatedly—that this hectic schedule improves as the puppy gets older.

HOME WITHIN A HOME

Your Puli puppy needs to be confined to one secure, puppy-proof area when no one is able to watch his every move. Generally the kitchen is the place of choice because the floor is washable. Likewise, it's a busy family area that will accustom the pup to a variety of noises, everything from pots and pans to the telephone, blender and dishwasher. He will also be enchanted by the smell of your cooking (and will never be

A treat or a favorite chew toy serves as motivator and reward for all types of training, from toilet training to enforcing house rules to teaching commands.

himself. With that schedule in mind, you can see that house-training a young puppy is not a part-time job. It requires someone to be home all day.

If that seems overwhelming or impossible, do a little planning. For example, plan to pick up your puppy at the start of a vacation period. If you can't get home in the middle of the day, plan to hire a dog-sitter or ask a neighbor

SHOULD WE ENROLL?

If you have the means and the time, you should definitely take your dog to obedience classes. Begin with puppy kindergarten classes in which puppies of all sizes learn basic lessons while getting the opportunity to meet and greet each other; it's as much about socialization as it is about good manners. What you learn in class you can practice at home. And if you goof up in practice, you'll get help in the next session.

CANINE DEVELOPMENT SCHEDULE

It is important to understand how and at what age a puppy develops into adulthood. If you are a puppy owner, consult this Canine Development Schedule to determine the stage of development your puppy is currently experiencing. This knowledge will help you as you work with the puppy in the weeks and months ahead.

PERIOD	AGE	CHARACTERISTICS
FIRST TO THIRD	BIRTH TO SEVEN WEEKS	Puppy needs food, sleep and warmth and responds to simple and gentle touching. Needs mother for security and disciplining. Needs littermates for learning and interacting with other dogs. Pup learns to function within a pack and learns pack order of dominance. Begin socializing pup with adults and children for short periods. Pup begins to become aware of his environment.
FOURTH	EIGHT TO TWELVE WEEKS	Brain is fully developed. Pup needs socializing with outside world. Remove from mother and littermates. Needs to change from canine pack to human pack. Human dominance necessary. Fear period occurs between 8 and 12 weeks. Avoid fright and pain.
FIFTH	THIRTEEN TO SIXTEEN WEEKS	Training and formal obedience should begin. Less association with other dogs, more with people, places, situations. Period will pass easily if you remember this is pup's change-to-adolescence time. Be firm and fair. Flight instinct prominent. Permissiveness and over-disciplining can do permanent damage. Praise for good behavior.
JUVENILE	FOUR TO EIGHT MONTHS	Another fear period about seven to eight months of age. It passes quickly, but be cautious of fright and pain. Sexual maturity reached. Dominant traits established. Dog should understand sit, down, come and stay by now.

NOTE: THESE ARE APPROXIMATE TIME FRAMES. ALLOW FOR INDIVIDUAL DIFFERENCES IN PUPPIES.

DAILY SCHEDULE

How many relief trips does your puppy need per day? A puppy up to the age of 14 weeks will need to go outside about 8 to 12 times per day! You will have to take the pup out any time he starts sniffing around the floor or turning in small circles, as well as after naps, meals, games and lessons or whenever he's released from his crate. Once the puppy is 14 to 22 weeks of age, he will require only 6 to 8 relief trips. At the ages of 22 to 32 weeks, the puppy will require about 5 to 7 trips. Adult dogs typically require 4 relief trips per day, in the morning, afternoon, evening and late at night.

critical when you burn something). An exercise pen (also called an "ex-pen," a puppy version of a playpen) within the room of choice is an excellent means of confinement for a young pup. The pen should be sturdy, with high sides, so that the pup cannot knock it down or climb out. He can see out and has a certain amount of space in which to run about, but he is safe from dangerous things like electrical cords, heating units, trash baskets or open kitchen-supply cabinets. Place the pen where the puppy will not get a blast of heat or air conditioning.

In the pen, you can put a few toys, his bed (which can be his crate if the dimensions of pen and crate are compatible) and a few layers of newspaper in one small corner, just in case. A water bowl can be hung at a convenient height on the side of the ex-pen so it won't become a splashing pool for an innovative puppy. His food dish can go on the floor, near but not under the water bowl.

Crates are something that pet owners are at last getting used to for their dogs. Wild or domestic canines have always preferred to sleep in den-like safe spots, and that is exactly what the crate provides. How often have you seen adult dogs that choose to sleep under a table or chair even though they have full run of the house? It's the den connection.

In your "happy" voice, use the word "Crate" every time you put the pup into his den. If he's new to a crate, toss in a small biscuit for him to chase the first few times. At night, after he's been outside, he should sleep in his crate. The crate may be kept in his designated area at night or, if you want to be sure to hear those wake-up yips in the morning, put the crate in a corner of your bedroom. However, don't make any response whatsoever to whining or crying. If he's completely ignored, he'll settle down and get to sleep.

Good bedding for a young puppy is an old folded bath towel or an old blanket, something that is easily washable and disposable if necessary ("accidents" will happen!). Never put newspaper in the puppy's crate. Also, those old ideas about adding a clock to replace his mother's heartbeat, or a hot-water bottle to replace her warmth, are just that—old ideas. The clock could drive the puppy nuts, and the hot-water bottle could end up as a very soggy waterbed! An extremely good breeder would have introduced your puppy to the crate by letting two pups sleep together for a couple of nights, followed by several nights alone. How thankful you will be if you found that breeder!

Safe toys in the pup's crate or area will keep him occupied, but monitor their condition closely. Discard any toys that show signs of being chewed to bits. Squeaky parts, bits of stuffing or plastic or any other small pieces can cause intestinal blockage or possibly choking if swallowed.

PROGRESSING WITH POTTY-TRAINING
After you've taken your puppy out and he has relieved himself

SOMEBODY TO BLAME

House-training a puppy can be frustrating for the puppy and the owner alike. The puppy does not instinctively understand the difference between defecating on the pavement outside and on the ceramic tile in the kitchen. He is confused and frightened by his human's exuberant reactions to his natural urges. The owner, arguably the more intelligent of the duo, is also frustrated that he cannot convince his puppy to obey his commands and instructions.

In frustration, the owner may struggle with the temptation to discipline the puppy, scold him or even strike him on the rear end. Harsh corrections are unnecessary and inappropriate, serving to defeat your purpose in gaining your puppy's trust and respect. Don't blame your nine-week-old puppy. Blame yourself for not being 100% consistent in the puppy's lessons and routine. The lesson here is simple: try harder and your puppy will succeed.

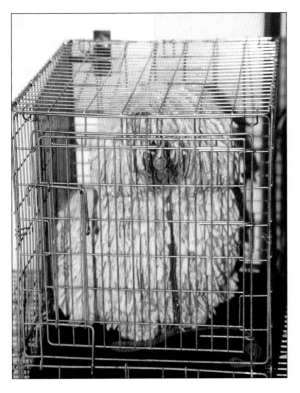

to prevent his first attempts to jump up onto the couch. The word to use in this case is "Off," not "Down." "Down" is the word you will use to teach the down position, which is something entirely different.

Most corrections at this stage come in the form of simply distracting the puppy. Instead of telling him "No" for "Don't chew the carpet," distract the chomping puppy with a toy and he'll forget about the carpet.

As you are playing with the pup, do not forget to watch him closely and pay attention to his body language. Whenever you see him begin to circle or sniff, take

Crate training has become a widely used method of housebreaking and training dogs. A wire crate, as shown here, is popular for use inside the home, as it affords the dog a view of what is going on around him.

in the area you've selected, he can have some free time with the family as long as there is someone responsible for watching him. That doesn't mean just someone in the same room who is watching TV or busy on the computer, but one person who is doing nothing other than keeping an eye on the pup, playing with him on the floor and helping him understand his position in the pack.

This first taste of freedom will let you begin to set the house rules. If you don't want the dog on the furniture, now is the time

TIDY BOY

Clean by nature, dogs do not like to soil their dens, which in effect are their crates or sleeping quarters. Unless not feeling well, dogs will not defecate or urinate in their crates. Crate training capitalizes on the dog's natural desire to keep his den clean. Be conscientious about giving the puppy as many opportunities to relieve himself outdoors as possible. Reward the puppy for correct behavior. Praise him and pet him whenever he "goes" in the correct location. Even the tidiest of puppies can have potty accidents, so be patient and dedicate more energy to helping your puppy achieve a clean lifestyle.

the puppy outside to relieve himself. If you are paper-training, put him back into his confined area on the newspapers. In either case, praise him as he eliminates while he actually is in the act of relieving himself. Three seconds after he has finished is too late! You'll be praising him for running toward you, picking up a toy or whatever he may be doing at that moment, and that's not what you want to be praising him for. Timing is a vital tool in all dog training. Use it.

Remove soiled newspapers immediately and replace them with clean ones. You may want to take a small piece of soiled paper and place it in the middle of the new clean papers, as the scent will attract him to that spot when it's time to go again. That scent attraction is why it's so important to clean up any messes made in the house by using a product specially made to eliminate the odor of dog urine and droppings. Regular household cleansers won't do the trick. Pet shops sell the best pet deodorizers. Invest in the largest container you can find.

Scent attraction eventually will lead your pup to his chosen spot outdoors; this is the basis of outdoor training. When you take your puppy outside to relieve himself, use a one-word command such as "Outside" or "Go-potty" (that's one word to the puppy!) as

TEACHER'S PET
Dogs are individuals, not robots, with many traits basic to their breed. Some, bred to work alone, are independent thinkers; others rely on you to call the shots. If you have enrolled in a training class, your instructor can offer alternative methods of training based on your individual dog's instincts and personality. You may benefit from using a different type of collar or switching to a class with different kinds of dogs.

you attach his leash. Then lead him to his spot. Now comes the hard part—hard for you, that is. Just stand there until he urinates and defecates. Move him a few feet in one direction or another if he's just sitting there looking at you, but remember that this is neither playtime nor time for a walk. This is strictly a business trip! Then, as he circles and

POTTY COMMAND

Most dogs love to please their masters; there are no bounds to what dogs will do to make their owners happy. The potty command is a good example of this theory. If toileting on command makes the master happy, then more power to him. Puppies will obligingly piddle if it really makes their keepers smile. Some owners can be creative about which word they will use to command their dogs to relieve themselves. Some popular choices are "Potty," "Tinkle," "Piddle," "Let's go," "Hurry up" and "Toilet." Give the command every time your puppy goes into position and the puppy will begin to associate his business with the command.

squats (remember your timing!), give him a quiet "Good dog" as praise. If you start to jump for joy, ecstatic over his performance, he'll do one of two things: either he will stop mid-stream, as it were, or he'll do it again for you—in the house—and expect you to be just as delighted!

Give him five minutes or so and, if he doesn't go in that time, take him back indoors to his confined area and try again in another ten minutes, or immediately if you see him sniffing and circling. By careful observation, you'll soon work out a successful schedule.

Accidents, by the way, are just that—accidents. Clean them up quickly and thoroughly, without comment, after the puppy has been taken outside to finish his business and then put back into his area or crate. If you witness an accident in progress, say "No!" in a stern voice and get the pup outdoors immediately. No punishment is needed. You and your puppy are just learning each other's language, and sometimes it's easy to miss a puppy's message. Chalk it up to experience and watch more closely from now on.

KEEPING THE PACK ORDERLY

Discipline is a form of training that brings order to life. For example, military discipline is what allows the soldiers in an army to work as one. Discipline is a form of teaching and, in dogs, is the basis of how the successful pack operates. Each member knows his place in the pack and all respect the leader, or alpha dog. It is essential for your puppy that you establish this type of relationship, with you as the alpha, or leader. It is a form of social coexistence that all canines recognize and accept. Discipline, therefore, is never to be confused with punishment. When you teach your puppy how you want him to behave, and he behaves properly and you praise him for it, you are disciplining him with a form of positive reinforcement.

For a dog, rewards come in the form of praise, a smile, a cheerful tone of voice, a few friendly pats or a rub of the ears. Rewards are also small food treats. Obviously, that does not mean bits of regular dog food. Instead, treats are very small bits of special things like cheese or pieces of soft dog treats. The idea is to reward the dog with something very small that he can taste and swallow, providing instant positive reinforcement. If he has to take time to chew the treat, he will have forgotten what he did to earn it by the time he is finished!

Your puppy should never be physically punished. The displeasure shown on your face and in your voice is sufficient to signal to the pup that he has done something wrong. He wants to please everyone higher up on the social ladder, especially his leader, so a

TIME TO PLAY!

Playtime can happen both indoors and out. A young puppy is growing so rapidly that he needs sleep more than he needs a lot of physical exercise. Puppies get sufficient exercise on their own just through normal puppy activity. Monitor play with young children so you can remove the puppy when he's had enough, or calm the kids if they get too rowdy. Almost all puppies love to chase after a toy you've thrown, and you can turn your games into educational activities. Every time your puppy brings the toy back to you, say "Give it" (or "Drop it") followed by "Good dog" and throwing it again. If he's reluctant to give it to you, offer a small treat so that he drops the toy as he takes the treat. He will soon get the idea.

The selection of the proper collar and lead is important for the safety and comfort of your Puli.

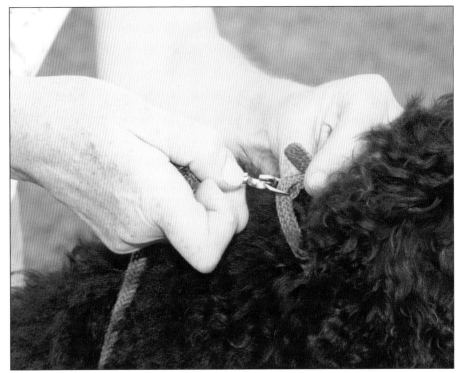

The selection of the proper collar and lead is important for the safety and comfort of your Puli.

scowl and harsh voice will take care of the error. Growling out the word "Shame!" when the pup is caught in the act of doing something wrong is better than the repetitive "No." Some dogs hear "No" so often that they begin to think it's their name! By the way, do not use the dog's name when you're correcting him. His name is reserved to get his attention for something pleasant about to take place.

There are punishments that have nothing to do with you. For example, your dog may think that chasing cats is one reason for his existence. You can try to stop it as much as you like but without success, because it's such fun for the dog. But one good hissing, spitting swipe of a cat's claws across the dog's nose will put an end to the game forever. Intervene

"SCHOOL" MODE

When is your puppy ready for a lesson? Maybe not always when you are. Attempting training with treats just before his mealtime is asking for disaster. Notice what times of day he performs best and make that Fido's school time.

only when your dog's eyeball is seriously at risk. Cat scratches can cause permanent damage to an innocent but annoying puppy.

PUPPY KINDERGARTEN

Collar and Lead

Pulik are quite determined and self-willed little creatures and will probably object to both collar and lead! A first step is to put on a lightweight collar for just a few minutes. After a few futile attempts to scratch it off, the pup will soon forget it and you can gradually increase the time that it is left on. The next step is to attach a light lead that the pup will probably not notice until you attempt to lead him along. The reaction will probably be like a little bucking bronco, but gentle coaxing words will surely help, coupled with gentle pulling to make the puppy accept that you are in charge.

After a while, your pup will stop pulling against you and should start to come along in the same direction. Soon he will accept that this collar and lead training can be fun, and he will start to trot alongside you. When your pup has built up sufficient immunity from his vaccinations, he will be ready for short walks outside the home area. It can be a great temptation to make early walks rather lengthy, as any proud owner will want to show off his new Puli. Please do remember that you have a very young animal that still has lots of growing to do, and that to overtire him will inhibit his growth.

When you embark on the first walk, choose somewhere that is comparatively quiet, with few diversions. Your pup will naturally be curious about the surroundings and need to gain confidence being in a strange place. To suddenly expose a pup to lots of people, traffic and other dogs can be rather overwhelming, so these outings should be taken

---

DON'T STRESS ME OUT

Your dog doesn't have to deal with paying the bills, the daily commute, PTA meetings and the like, but, believe it or not, there's a lot of stress in a dog's world. Stress can be caused by the owner's impatient demeanor and his angry or harsh corrections. If your dog cringes when you reach for his training collar, he's stressed. An older dog is sometimes stressed out when he goes to a new home. No matter what the cause, put off all training until he's over it. If he's going through a fear period—shying away from people, trembling when spoken to, avoiding eye contact or hiding under furniture—wait to resume training. Naturally you'd also postpone your lessons if the dog were sick, and the same goes for you. Show some compassion.

ATTENTION

You've been using the dog's name since the minute you collected him from the breeder, so you should be able to get his attention by saying his name—with a big smile and in an excited tone of voice. His response will be the puppy equivalent of "Here I am! What are we going to do?" Your immediate response (if you haven't guessed by now) is "Good dog." Rewarding him at the moment he pays attention to you teaches him the proper way to respond when he hears his name.

LEASH TRAINING

House-training and leash training go hand in hand, literally. When taking your puppy outside to do his business, lead him there on his leash. Unless an emergency potty run is called for, do not whisk the puppy up into your arms and take him outside. If you have a fenced yard, you have the advantage of letting the puppy loose to go out, but it's better to put the dog on the leash and take him to his designated place in the yard until he is reliably house-trained. Taking the puppy for a walk is the best way to house-train a dog. The dog will associate the walk with his time to relieve himself, and the exercise of walking stimulates the dog's bowels and bladder. Dogs that are not trained to relieve themselves on a walk may hold it until they get back home, which of course defeats half the purpose of the walk.

Well-timed treats and praise help your dog to make the connection between your words and the desired response. calmly and in quiet places. Let the pup become confident and gradually encounter diversions. While you are walking, he will eventually come to see other dogs being walked. Don't allow him to dash across to them, as some will try. You will have no idea of the reactions of the other dogs, which could be protective or aggressive.

EXERCISES FOR A BASIC CANINE EDUCATION

THE SIT EXERCISE

There are several ways to teach the puppy to sit. The first one is to catch him whenever he is about to sit and, as his backside nears the floor, say "Sit, good dog!" That's positive reinforcement and, if your timing is sharp, he will learn that what he's doing at that second is connected to your saying "Sit" and that you think he's clever for doing it!

Another method is to start with the puppy on his leash in front of you. Show him a treat in the palm of your right hand. Bring your hand up under his nose and, almost in slow motion, move your hand up and back so his nose goes up in the air and his head tilts back as he follows the treat in your hand. At that point, he will have to either sit or fall over, so as his back legs buckle under, say "Sit, good dog," and then give him the treat and lots of praise. You may have to begin with your hand lightly running up his chest, actually lifting his chin up until he sits. Some (usually older) dogs require gentle pressure on their hindquarters with the left hand, in which case the dog should be on your left side. Puppies generally do not appreciate this physical dominance.

After a few times, you should be able to show the dog a treat in the open palm of your hand, raise

READY, SIT, GO!
On your marks, get set: train! Most professional trainers agree that the sit command is the place to start your dog's formal education. Sitting is a natural posture for most dogs, and they respond to the sit exercise willingly and readily. For every lesson, begin with the sit command so that you start out with a successful exercise; likewise, you should practice the sit command at the end of every lesson as well, because you always want to end on a high note.

your hand waist-high as you say "Sit" and have him sit. You will thereby have taught him two things at the same time. Both the verbal command and the motion of the hand are signals for the sit. Your puppy is watching you almost more than he is listening to you, so what you do is just as important as what you say.

Your pup will plop into a sit on his own many times throughout the day. Reinforce the command by using the word "sit" whenever you see him go into the sit position.

Don't save any of these drills only for training sessions. Use them as much as possible at odd times during a normal day. The dog should always sit before being given his food dish. He should sit to let you go through a doorway first, when the doorbell rings or when you stop to speak to someone on the street.

THE DOWN EXERCISE

Before beginning to teach the down command, you must consider how the dog feels about this exercise. To him, "down" is a submissive position. Being flat on the floor with you standing over him is not his idea of fun. It's up to you to let him know that, while it may not be fun, the reward of your approval is worth his effort.

Start with the puppy on your left side in a sit position. Hold the leash right above his collar in your left hand. Have an extra-special treat, such as a small piece of cooked chicken or hot dog, in your right hand. Place it at the end of the pup's nose and steadily move your hand down and forward along the ground. Hold the leash to prevent a sudden lunge for the food. As the puppy goes into the down position, say "Down" very gently.

The difficulty with this exercise is twofold: it's both the submissive aspect and the fact that most people say the word "Down" as if they were drill sergeants in charge of recruits! So issue the command sweetly, give him the treat and have the pup maintain the down position for several seconds. If he tries to get up immediately, place your hands on his shoulders and press down gently, giving him a very quiet

KEEP IT SIMPLE—AND FUN
Keep your lessons simple, interesting and user-friendly. Fun breaks help you both. Spend two minutes or ten teaching your puppy, but practice only as long as your dog enjoys what he's doing and is focused on pleasing you. If he's bored or distracted, stop the training session after any correct response (always end on a high note!). After a few minutes of playtime, you can go back to "hitting the books."

"Good dog." As you progress with this lesson, increase the "down time" until he will hold it until you say "Okay" (his cue for release). Practice this one in the house at various times throughout the day.

By increasing the length of time during which the dog must maintain the down position, you'll find many uses for it. For example, he can lie at your feet in the vet's office or anywhere that both of you have to wait, when you are on the phone, while the family is eating and so forth. If you progress to training for competitive obedience, he'll already be all set for the exercise called the "long down."

THE STAY EXERCISE

You can teach your Puli to stay in the sit, down and stand positions. To teach the sit/stay, have the dog sit on your left side. Hold the leash at waist level in your left hand and let the dog know that you have a treat in your closed right hand. Step forward on your right foot as you say "Stay." Immediately turn and stand directly in front of the dog, keeping your right hand up high so he'll keep his eye on the treat hand and maintain the sit position for a count of five. Return to your original position and offer the reward.

Increase the length of the sit/stay each time until the dog can hold it for at least 30 seconds without moving. After about a week of success, move out on your right foot and take two steps before turning to face the dog. Give the "Stay" hand signal (left palm back toward the dog's head) as you leave. He gets the treat when you return and he holds the sit/stay. Increase the distance that you walk away from him before turning until you reach the length of your training leash. But don't

DOWN

"Down" is a harsh-sounding word and a submissive posture in dog body language, thus presenting two obstacles in teaching the down command. When the dog is about to flop down on his own, tell him "Good down." Pups that are not good about being handled learn better by having food lowered in front of them. A dog that trusts you can be gently guided into position. When you give the command "Down," be sure to say it sweetly!

into your original position. While you are training, it's okay to murmur something like "Hold on" to encourage him to stay put. When the dog will stay without moving when you are at a distance of 3 or 4 feet, begin to increase the length of time before you return. Be sure he holds the down on your return until you say "Okay." At that point, he gets his treat—just so he'll remember for next time that it's not over until it's over.

THE COME EXERCISE

No command is more important to the safety of your Puli than "Come." It is what you should say every single time you see the puppy running toward you: "Ziggy, come! Good dog." During playtime, run a few feet away from the puppy and turn and tell

The pup's coming to you should always result in something good for him—a treat, praise, petting, a toy, etc. If coming to you is enjoyable for him, he should want to come when you call him.

rush it! Go back to the beginning if he moves before he should. No matter what the lesson, never be upset by having to back up for a few days. The repetition and practice are what will make your dog reliable in these commands. It won't do any good to move on to something more difficult if the command is not mastered at the easier levels. Above all, even if you do get frustrated, never let your puppy know. Always keep a positive, upbeat attitude during training, which will transmit to your dog for positive results.

The down/stay is taught in the same way once the dog is completely reliable and steady with the down command. Again, don't rush it. With the dog in the down position on your left side, step out on your right foot as you say "Stay." Return by walking around in back of the dog and

---

I WILL FOLLOW YOU

Obedience isn't just a classroom activity. In your home you have many great opportunities to teach your dog polite manners. Allowing your pet on the bed or furniture elevates him to your level, which is not a good idea (the word is "Off!"). Use the "umbilical cord" method, keeping your dog on lead so he has to go with you wherever you go. You sit, he sits. You walk, he heels. You stop, he sit-stays. Everywhere you go, he's with you, but you go first!

him to "Come" as he is already running to you. You can go so far as to teach your puppy two things at once if you squat down and hold out your arms. As the pup gets close to you and you're saying "Good dog," bring your right arm in about waist high. Now he's also learning the hand signal, an excellent device should you be on the phone when you need to get him to come to you! You'll also both be one step ahead when you enter obedience classes.

When the puppy responds to your well-timed "Come," try it with the puppy on the training leash. This time, catch him off guard, while he's sniffing a leaf or watching a bird: "Ziggy, come!" You may have to pause for a split second after his name to be sure you have his attention. If the puppy shows any sign of confusion, give the leash a mild jerk and take a couple of steps backward. Do not repeat the command. In this case, you should say "Good come" as he reaches you.

That's the number-one rule of training. Each command word is given just once. Anything more is nagging. You'll also notice that all commands are one word only. Even when they are actually two words, you say them as one.

Never call the dog to come to you—with or without his name—if you are angry or intend to correct him for some misbehavior.

When correcting the pup, you go to him. Your dog must always connect "Come" with something pleasant and with your approval; then you can rely on his response.

Puppies, like children, have notoriously short attention spans, so don't overdo it with any of the training. Keep each lesson short.

COME AND GET IT!

The come command is your dog's safety signal. Until he is 99% perfect in responding, don't use the come command if you cannot enforce it. Practice on leash with treats or squeakers, or whenever the dog is running to you. Never call him to come to you if he is to be corrected for a misdemeanor. Reward the dog with a treat and happy praise whenever he comes to you.

ing to smile at you) with a look that says "Make me!" Laugh, throw his favorite toy and skip the lesson you had planned. Pups will be pups!

THE HEEL EXERCISE

The second most important command to teach, after the come, is the heel. When you are walking your growing puppy, you need to be in control. Besides, it looks terrible to be pulled and yanked down the street, and it's not much fun either. Your eight- to ten-week-old puppy will probably follow you everywhere, but that's his natural instinct, not your control over the situation. However, any time he does follow you, you can say "Heel" and be ahead of the game, as he will learn to associate this command with the action of following you before you even begin teaching him to heel.

It takes practice and persistence to teach a curious pup to walk politely by your side. Keep at it and stay positive!

Break it up with a quick run around the yard or a ball toss, repeat the lesson and quit as soon as the pup gets it right. That way, you will always end with a "Good dog."

Life isn't perfect and neither are puppies. A time will come, often around ten months of age, when he'll become "selectively deaf" or choose to "forget" his name. He may respond by wagging his tail (and even seem-

OKAY!

This is the signal that tells your dog that he can quit whatever he was doing. Use "Okay" to end a session on a correct response to a command. (Never end on an incorrect response.) Lots of praise follows. People use "Okay" a lot and it has other uses for dogs, too. Your dog is barking. You say, "Okay! Come!" "Okay" signals him to stop the barking activity and "Come" allows him to come to you for a "Good dog."

There is a very precise, almost military, procedure for teaching your dog to heel. As with all other obedience training, begin with the dog on your left side. He will be in a very nice sit and you will have the training leash across your chest. Hold the loop and folded leash in your right hand. Pick up the slack leash above the dog in your left hand and hold it loosely at your side. Step out on your left foot as you say "Heel." If the puppy does not move, give a gentle tug or pat your left leg to get him started. If he surges ahead of you, stop and pull him back gently until he is at your side. Tell him to sit and begin again.

Walk a few steps and stop while the puppy is correctly beside you. Tell him to sit and give mild verbal praise. (More enthusiastic praise will encourage him to think the lesson is over.) Repeat the lesson, increasing the number of steps you take only as long as the dog is heeling nicely beside you. When you end the lesson, have him hold the sit, then give him the "Okay" to let him know that this is the end of the lesson. Praise him so that he knows he did a good job.

The cure for excessive pulling (a common problem) is to stop when the dog is no more than 2 or 3 feet ahead of you. Guide him back into position and begin again. With a really determined puller, try switching to a head

collar. When used correctly, this will automatically turn the pup's head toward you so you can bring him back easily to the heel posi-

LET'S GO!

Many people use "Let's go" instead of "Heel" when teaching their dogs to behave on lead. It sounds more like fun! When beginning to teach the heel, whatever command you use, always step off on your left foot. That's the one next to the dog, who is on your left side, in case you've forgotten. Keep a loose leash. When the dog pulls ahead, stop, bring him back and begin again. Use treats to guide him around turns.

know whether he'll get a treat or not, but he should keep performing well just in case! Finally, you will stop giving treat rewards entirely. Save them for something brand-new that you want to teach him. Keep up the praise and you'll always have a "good dog."

OBEDIENCE CLASSES
The advantages of an obedience class are that your dog will have to learn amid the distractions of other people and dogs and that your mistakes will be quickly corrected by the trainer. Teaching

Only progress to off-leash training in a safely enclosed area and only once the exercise has been learned reliably on lead.

tion. Give quiet, reassuring praise every time the leash goes slack and he's staying with you.

Staying and heeling can take a lot out of a dog, so provide play-time and free-running exercise to shake off the stress when the lessons are over. You don't want him to associate training with all work and no fun.

TAPERING OFF TIDBITS
Your dog has been watching you—and the hand that treats—throughout all of his lessons, and now it's time to break the treat habit. Begin by giving him treats at the end of each lesson only. Then start to give a treat after the end of only some of the lessons. At the end of every lesson, as well as during the lessons, be consistent with the praise. Your pup now doesn't

TIPS FOR TRAINING AND SAFETY
1. Whether on or off leash, practice only in a fenced area.
2. Remove the training collar when the training session is over.
3. Don't try to break up a dogfight.
4. "Come," "Leave it" and "Wait" are safety commands.
5. The dog belongs in a crate or behind a barrier when riding in the car.
6. Don't ignore the dog's first sign of aggression. Aggression only gets worse, so take it seriously.
7. Keep the faces of children and dogs separated.
8. Pay attention to what the dog is chewing.
9. Keep the vet's number near your phone.
10. "Okay" is a useful release command.

your dog along with a qualified instructor and other handlers who may have more dog experience than you is another plus of the class environment. The instructor and other handlers can help you to find the most efficient way of teaching your dog a command or exercise. It's often easier to learn by other people's mistakes than your own. You will also learn all of the requirements for competitive obedience trials, in which you can earn titles and go on to advanced jumping and retrieving exercises, which are fun for many dogs. Obedience classes build the foundation needed for many other canine activities (in which we humans are allowed to participate, too!).

TRAINING FOR OTHER ACTIVITIES

Once your dog has basic obedience under his collar and is 12 months of age, you can enter the world of agility training. Dogs think agility is pure fun, like being turned loose in an amusement park full of obstacles! In addition to agility, there are also tracking tests; both of these events are open to all breeds. Puli owners may want to develop and test their dogs' instincts with herding events, participating along with other herding breeds. For those who like to volunteer, there is the wonderful feeling of owning a therapy dog and visiting

Your Puli will dance for joy if you provide him with a good education and lots of opportunity for activity and fun with you.

hospices, nursing homes and veterans' homes to bring smiles, comfort and companionship to those who live there.

Around the house, your Puli can be taught to do some simple chores. You might teach him to carry household items or fetch the morning newspaper. The kids can teach the dog all kinds of tricks, from playing hide-and-seek to balancing a biscuit on his nose. A family dog is what rounds out the family. Everything he does, including sitting at your feet and gazing lovingly at you, represents the bonus of owning a dog.

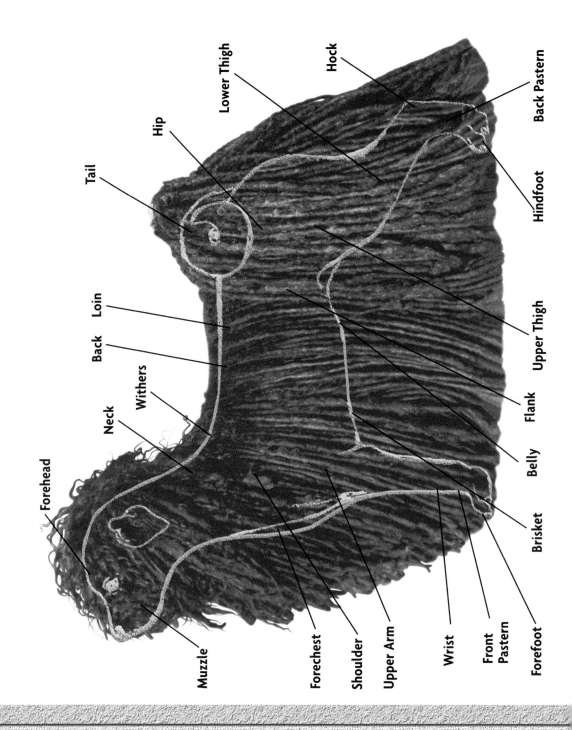

Lower Thigh

Hock

Back Pastern

Hip

Hindfoot

Tail

Upper Thigh

Loin

Back

Flank

Withers

Neck

Belly

Forehead

Brisket

Muzzle

Forechest

Shoulder

Upper Arm

Wrist

Front Pastern

Forefoot

PHYSICAL STRUCTURE OF THE PULI

HEALTHCARE OF YOUR

PULI

By Lowell Ackerman, DVM, DACVD

The Puli is certainly among the healthiest breeds in dogdom. They typically need to see the vet only once a year for their physical exams, booster shots and a new supply of heartworm and flea/tick preventives. The best route to a healthy dog is starting out with a well-bred, sound puppy and keeping up with routine maintenance tasks at home, including dental care, ear cleaning, grooming and proper feeding.

Before you buy a dog, meet and interview the veterinarians in your area. Take everything into consideration: discuss background, specialties, fees, emergency policies, etc.

HEALTHCARE FOR A LIFETIME

When you own a dog, you become his healthcare advocate over his entire lifespan, as well as being the one to shoulder the financial burden of such care. Accordingly, it is worthwhile to focus on prevention rather than treatment, as you and your pet will both be happier.

Of course, the best place to have begun your program of preventive healthcare is with the initial purchase or adoption of your dog. There is no way of guaranteeing that your new furry friend is free of medical problems, but there are some things you can do to improve your odds. You certainly should have done

adequate research into the Puli and have selected your puppy carefully rather than buying on impulse. Health issues aside, a large number of pet abandonment and relinquishment cases arise from a mismatch between pet needs and owner expectations. This is entirely preventable with appropriate planning and finding a good breeder.

Regarding healthcare issues specifically, it is very difficult to make blanket statements about where to acquire a problem-free pet, but, again, a reputable breeder is your best bet. In an ideal situation you have the opportunity to see both parents, get references from other owners of the breeder's pups and see

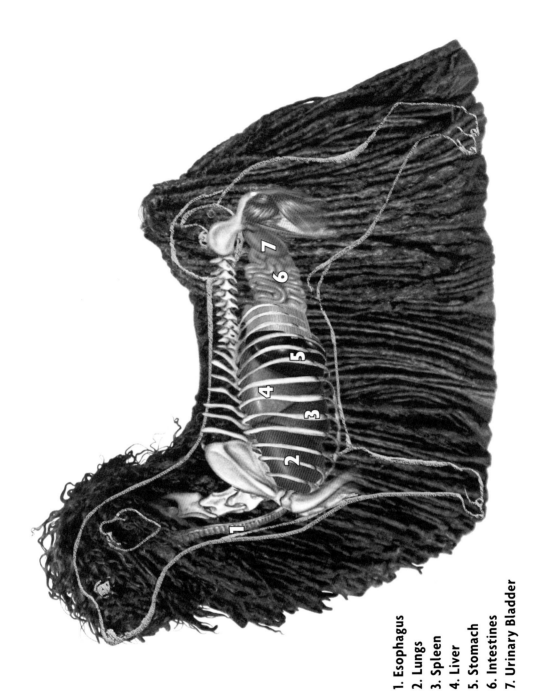

1. Esophagus
2. Lungs
3. Spleen
4. Liver
5. Stomach
6. Intestines
7. Urinary Bladder

INTERNAL ORGANS OF THE PULI

genetic-testing documentation for several generations of the litter's ancestors. At the very least, you must thoroughly investigate the Puli and the problems inherent in that breed, as well as the genetic testing available to screen for those problems. Genetic testing offers some important benefits, but is available for only a few disorders in a relatively small number of breeds and is not available for some of the most common genetic diseases, such as hip dysplasia, cataracts, epilepsy, cardiomyopathy, etc. This area of research is indeed exciting and increasingly important, and advances will continue to be made each year. In fact, recent research has shown that there is an equivalent dog gene for 75% of known human genes, so research done in either species is likely to benefit the other. In the meantime, tests like eye exams and x-rays are available to screen breeding stocks and good breeders will have these tests performed.

We've also discussed that evaluating the behavioral nature of your Puli and that of his immediate family members is an important part of the selection process that cannot be underestimated or overemphasized. It is sometimes difficult to evaluate temperament in puppies because certain behavioral tendencies, such as some forms of aggression, may not be immediately evident. More dogs are euthanized each year for behavioral reasons than for all medical conditions combined, so it is critical to take temperament issues seriously. Start with a well-balanced, friendly companion and put the time and effort into proper socialization, and you will both be rewarded with a lifelong valued relationship.

Assuming that you have started off with a pup from healthy, sound stock, you then become responsible for helping your veterinarian keep your pet healthy. Some crucial things happen before you even bring your puppy home. Parasite control typically begins at two weeks of age, and vaccinations typically begin at six to eight weeks of age. A pre-pubertal evaluation is typically scheduled for about six months of age. At this time, a dental evaluation is done (since the adult teeth are now in), heartworm prevention is started and neutering or spaying is most commonly done.

It is critical to commence regular dental care at home if you have not already done so. It may not sound very important, but most dogs have active periodontal disease by four years of age if they don't have their teeth cleaned regularly at home, not just at their veterinary exams. Dental problems lead to more than just bad "doggy breath." Gum disease can have very serious medical conse-

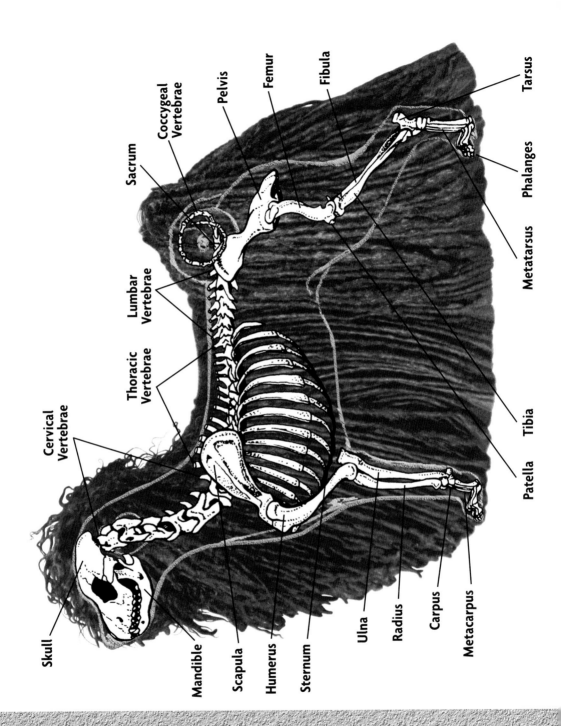

Coccygeal
Vertebrae

Pelvis

Femur

Fibula

Tarsus

Sacrum

Phalanges

Metatarsus

Lumbar
Vertebrae

Thoracic
Vertebrae

Tibia

Cervical
Vertebrae

Patella

Skull

Mandible

Scapula

Humerus

Sternum

Ulna

Radius

Carpus

Metacarpus

Skeletal Structure of the Puli

quences. If you start brushing your dog's teeth and using antiseptic rinses from a young age, your dog will be accustomed to it and will not resist. The results will be healthy dentition, which your pet will need to enjoy a long, healthy life.

Most dogs are considered adults at a year of age, although some larger breeds still have some filling out to do up to about two or so years old. Even individual dogs within each breed have different healthcare requirements, so work with your veterinarian to determine what will be needed and what your role should be. This doctor-client relationship is important, because as vaccination guidelines change, there may not be an annual "vaccine visit" scheduled. You must make sure that you see your veterinarian at least annually, even if no vaccines are due, because this is the best opportunity to coordinate health-care activities and to make sure that no medical issues creep by unaddressed.

When your Puli reaches about seven or eight years old, or as recommended by the vet, he is considered a "senior" and should start a preventive senior-care program. In general, if you've been taking great care of your canine companion throughout his formative and adult years, the transition to senior status should be a smooth one. Age is not a

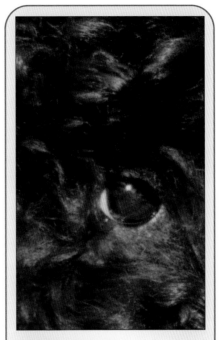

CHECK HIS EYES
Do check your Puli's eyes every single day. Nature's way of cleaning is a slight watery discharge should any dust or foreign matter cause irritation. This is likely to accumulate in the corner of the eye, where it will dry out into a hard clump. If neglected, this can lead to a gumming up with resultant soreness.

disease, and as long as everything is functioning as it should, there is no reason why most of late adulthood should not be rewarding for both you and your pet. This is especially true if you have tended to the details, such as regular veterinary visits, proper dental care, excellent nutrition and management of bone and joint issues.

YOUR DOG NEEDS TO VISIT THE VET IF:

- He has ingested a toxin such as antifreeze or a toxic plant; in these cases, administer first aid and call the vet right away
- His teeth are discolored, loose or missing or he has sores or other signs of infection or abnormality in the mouth
- He has been vomiting, has had diarrhea or has been constipated for over 24 hours; call immediately if you notice blood
- He has refused food for over 24 hours
- His eating habits, water intake or toilet habits have noticeably changed; if you have noticed weight gain or weight loss
- He shows symptoms of bloat, which requires *immediate* attention
- He is salivating excessively
- He has a lump in his throat
- He has a lump or bumps anywhere on the body
- He is very lethargic
- He appears to be in pain or otherwise has trouble chewing or swallowing
- His skin loses elasticity

Of course, there will be other instances in which a visit to the vet is necessary; these are just some of the signs that could be indicative of serious problems that need to be caught as early as possible.

At the senior stage in your Puli's life, your veterinarian will likely schedule visits twice yearly, instead of once, to run some laboratory screenings, electrocardiograms and the like, and to change the diet to something more digestible. Catching problems early is the best way to manage them effectively. Treating the early stages of heart disease is so much easier than trying to intervene when there is more significant damage to the heart muscle. Similarly, managing the beginning of kidney problems is fairly routine if there is no significant kidney damage. Other problems, like cognitive dysfunction (similar to senility and Alzheimer's disease), cancer, diabetes and arthritis, are more common in older dogs, but all can be treated to help the dog live as many happy, comfortable years as possible. Just as in people, medical management is more effective (and less expensive) when you catch things early.

SELECTING A VETERINARIAN

There is probably no more important decision that you will make regarding your pet's healthcare than the selection of his doctor. Your pet's veterinarian will be a pediatrician, family-practice physician and gerontologist, depending on the dog's life stage, and will be the individual who makes recommendations regarding issues such as when specialists need to be consulted, when diagnostic testing and/or therapeutic intervention is needed and when you will need to seek outside emergency and critical-care services. Your vet will act as your advocate and liaison throughout these processes.

Everyone has his own idea about what to look for in a vet, an individual who will play a big role in his dog's (and, of course, his own) life for many years to come. For some, it is the compassionate caregiver with whom they hope to develop a professional relationship to span the lives of their dogs and even their future pets. For others, they are seeking a clinician with keen diagnostic and therapeutic insight who can deliver state-of-the-art healthcare. Still others need a veterinary facility that is open evenings and weekends, is in close proximity or provides mobile veterinary services to accommodate their schedules; these people may not much mind that their dogs might see different veterinarians on each visit. Just as we have different reasons for selecting our own healthcare professionals (e.g., covered by insurance plan, expert in field, convenient location, etc.), we should not expect that there is a one-size-fits-all recommendation for selecting a veterinarian and veterinary practice. The best advice is to be honest in your assessment of what you expect

BEWARE THE SPIDER

Should you worry about having a spider spinning her mucilaginous web over your dog? Like other venomous critters, spiders can bite dogs and cause severe reactions. The most deleterious eight-leggers are the black and red widow spiders, brown recluse and common brown spiders, whose bites can cause local pain, cramping, spasms and restlessness. These signals tell owners there is a problem, as the bites themselves can be difficult to locate under your dog's coat. Another vicious arachnid is the bark scorpion, whose bite can cause excessive drooling, tearing, urination and defecation. Often spider and scorpion bites are misdiagnosed because vets don't recognize the signs and owners didn't witness the escape of the avenging arachnid.

from a veterinary practice and to conscientiously research the options in your area. You will quickly appreciate that not all veterinary practices are the same, and you will be happiest with one that truly meets your needs.

There is another point to be considered in the selection of veterinary services. Not that long ago, a single veterinarian would attempt to manage all medical and surgical issues as they arose. That was often problematic, because veterinarians are trained in many species and many diseases, and it was just impossible for general veterinary practitioners to be experts in every species, every breed, every field and every ailment. However, just as in the human healthcare fields, specialization has allowed general practitioners to concentrate on primary healthcare delivery, especially wellness and the prevention of infectious diseases, and to utilize a network of specialists to assist in the management of conditions that require specific expertise and experience. Thus there are now many types of veterinary specialists, including dermatologists, cardiologists, ophthalmologists, surgeons, internists, oncologists, neurologists, behaviorists, criticalists and others to help primary-care veterinarians deal with complicated medical challenges. In most cases, specialists see cases referred by primary-care veterinarians, make diagnoses and set up management plans. From there, the animals' ongoing care is returned to their primary-care veterinarians. This important team approach to your pet's medical-care needs has provided opportunities for advanced care and an unparalleled level of quality to be delivered.

With all of the opportunities for your Puli to receive high-quality veterinary medical care, there is another topic that needs to be addressed at the same time—cost. It's been said that you can have

excellent healthcare or inexpensive healthcare, but never both; this is as true in veterinary medicine as it is in human medicine. While veterinary costs are a fraction of what the same services cost in the human healthcare arena, it is still difficult to deal with unanticipated medical costs, especially since they can easily creep into hundreds or even thousands of dollars if specialists or emergency services become involved. However, there are ways of managing these risks. The easiest is to buy pet health insurance and realize that its foremost purpose is not to cover routine healthcare visits but rather to serve as an umbrella for those rainy days when your pet needs medical care and you don't want to worry about whether or not you can afford that care.

Pet insurance policies are very cost-effective (and very inexpensive by human health-insurance standards), but make sure that you buy the policy long before you intend to use it (preferably starting in puppyhood, because coverage will exclude pre-existing conditions) and that you are actually buying an indemnity insurance plan from an insurance company that is regulated by your state or province. Many insurance policy look-alikes are actually discount clubs that are redeemable only at specific locations and for specific services. An indemnity plan covers your pet at almost all veterinary, specialty and emergency practices and is an excellent way to manage your pet's ongoing healthcare needs.

VACCINATIONS AND INFECTIOUS DISEASES

There has never been an easier time to prevent a variety of infectious diseases in your dog, but the advances we've made in veterinary medicine come with a price—choice. Now while this choice is a good thing, it also has never been more difficult for the pet owner (or the veterinarian) to make an informed decision about the best way to protect pets through vaccination.

Years ago, it was just accepted that puppies got a starter series of vaccinations and then annual "boosters" throughout their lives to keep them protected. As more and more vaccines became available, consumers wanted the convenience of having all of that protection in a single injection. The result was "multivalent" vaccines that crammed a lot of protection into a single syringe. The manufacturers' recommendations were to give the vaccines annually, and this was a simple enough protocol to follow. However, as veterinary medicine has become more sophisticated and we have started looking more at healthcare quandaries rather

COMMON PULI PROBLEMS

Pulik experience a number of common problems that can be managed by their owners. Bad breath, though uncommon, requires that the owner check the dog's mouth. Decayed teeth should be removed, as they can cause bad breath and poison the digestive system. Prevent tooth decay by providing proper chewing devices and by having your veterinarian clean your dog's teeth annually or semi-annually in addition to your regular toothbrushing at home.

Diarrhea can be caused by overfeeding, the wrong type of food or too-rich food. Withholding food is the first step and then giving small drinks of cooled boiled water to which you may add a little glucose and a pinch of salt to assist rehydration. If the problem does not clear up within 24 hours, consult your vet.

Grass seeds can be an annual problem with heavily coated breeds. They can penetrate the skin if not detected, tending to collect on the head and around the eyes due to the Puli's natural curiosity and sniffing around when being walked. Another vulnerable spot for grass seeds is between the toes. If left undetected, they could lead to the formation of an abscess.

than convenience, it became necessary to reevaluate the situation and deal with some tough questions. It is important to realize that whether or not to use a particular vaccine depends on the risk of contracting the disease against which it protects, the severity of the disease if it is contracted, the duration of immunity provided by the vaccine, the safety of the product and the needs of the individual animal. In a very general sense, rabies, distemper, hepatitis and parvovirus are considered core vaccine needs, while parainfluenza, *Bordetella bronchiseptica*, leptospirosis, coronavirus and borreliosis (Lyme disease) are considered non-core needs and best reserved for animals that demonstrate reasonable risk of contracting the diseases.

THE GREAT VACCINATION DEBATE

What kinds of questions need to be addressed? When the vet injects multiple organisms at the same time, might some of the components interfere with one another in the development of immunologic protection? We don't have the comprehensive answer for that question, but it does appear that the immune system better handles agents when given individually. Unfortunately, most manufacturers still bundle their vaccine components because that is what

most pet owners want, so getting vaccines with single components can sometimes be difficult.

Another question has to do with how often vaccines should be given. Again, this seems to be different for each vaccine component. There seems to be a general consensus that a puppy (or a dog with an unknown vaccination history) should get a series of vaccinations to initially stimulate his immunity and then a booster at one year of age, but even the veterinary associations and colleges have trouble reaching agreement about what he should get after that. Rabies vaccination schedules are not debated, because vaccine schedules for this contagious and devastating disease are determined by government agencies. Regarding the rest, some recommend that we continue to give the vaccines annually because this method has worked well as a disease preventive for decades and delivers predictable protection. Others recommend that some of the vaccines need to be given only every second or third year, as this can be done without affecting levels of protection. This is probably true for some vaccine components (such as hepatitis), but there have been no large studies to demonstrate what the optimal interval should be and whether the same principles hold true for all breeds.

It may be best to just measure titers, which are protective blood levels of various vaccine components, on an annual basis, but that too is not without controversy. Scientists have not precisely determined the minimum titer of specific vaccine components that will be guaranteed to provide a pet with protection. Pets with very high titers will clearly be protected and those with very low titers will need repeat vaccinations, but there is also a large "gray zone" of pets that probably have intermediate protection and may or may not need repeat vaccination, depending on their risk of coming into contact with the disease.

These questions leave primary-care veterinarians in a very uncomfortable position, one that is not easy to resolve. Do they recommend annual vaccination in a manner that has demonstrated successful protection for decades, do they recommend skipping vaccines some years and hope that the protection lasts or do they measure blood tests (titers) and hope that the results are convincing enough to clearly indicate whether repeat vaccination is warranted?

These aren't the only vaccination questions impacting pets, owners and veterinarians. Other controversies focus on whether vaccines should be dosed according to body weight (currently they

PROBLEM: AND THAT STARTS WITH "P"

Urinary tract problems more commonly affect female dogs, especially those who have been spayed. The first sign that a urinary tract problem exists usually is a strong odor from the urine or an unusual color. Blood in the urine, known as hematuria, is another sign of an infection, related to cystitis, a bladder infection, bladder cancer or a blood-clotting disorder. Urinary tract problems can also be signaled by the dog's straining while urinating, experiencing pain during urination and genital discharge as well as excessive water intake and urination.

Excessive drinking, in and of itself, does not indicate a urinary tract problem. A dog who is drinking more than normal may have a kidney or liver problem, a hormonal disorder or diabetes mellitus. Behaviorists report a disorder known as psychogenic polydipsia, which manifests itself in excessive drinking and urination. If you notice your dog drinking much more than normal, take him to the vet.

are administered in uniform doses, regardless of the animal's size), whether there are breed-specific issues important in determining vaccination programs (for instance, we know that some breeds react badly to the leptospirosis vaccine and some have a harder time mounting an appropriate immune response to the parvovirus vaccine and might benefit from a different dose or injection interval) and which type of vaccine—live-virus or inactivated—offers more advantages with fewer disadvantages. Clearly, there are many more questions than there are answers. The important thing, as a pet owner, is to be aware of the issues and be able to work with your veterinarian to make decisions that are right for your pet. Be an informed consumer and you will appreciate the deliberation required in tailoring a vaccination program to best meet the needs of your pet. Expect also that this is an ongoing, ever-changing topic of debate; thus, the decisions you make this year won't necessarily be the same as the ones you make next year.

NEUTERING/SPAYING

Sterilization procedures (neutering for males/spaying for females) are meant to accomplish several purposes. While the underlying premise is to address the risk of pet overpopulation, there are also some medical and behavioral benefits to the surgeries. For females, spaying prior to the first estrus (heat cycle) leads to a marked reduction in the risk of mammary cancer and other serious female problems. There also will be no manifestations of "heat" to attract male dogs and no bleeding in the house. For males, there is prevention of testicular cancer and a reduction in the risk of prostate problems. In both sexes there may be some limited reduction in aggressive behaviors toward other dogs, and some diminishing of urine marking, roaming and mounting.

While neutering and spaying do indeed prevent animals from contributing to pet overpopulation, even no-cost and low-cost neutering options have not eliminated the problem. Perhaps one of the main reasons for this is that individuals that intentionally breed their dogs and those that allow their animals to run at large are the main causes of unwanted offspring. Also, animals in shelters are often there because they were abandoned or relinquished, not because they came from unplanned matings. Neutering/spaying is important, but it should be considered in the context of the real causes of animals' ending up in shelters and eventually being euthanized.

One of the important considerations regarding neutering is that it is a surgical procedure.

This sometimes gets lost in discussions of low-cost procedures and commoditization of the process. In females, spaying is specifically referred to as an ovariohysterectomy. In this procedure, a midline incision is made in the abdomen and the entire uterus and both ovaries are surgically removed. While this is a major invasive surgical procedure, it usually has few complications because it is typically performed on healthy young animals. However, it is major surgery, as any woman who has had a hysterectomy will attest.

In males, neutering has traditionally referred to castration, which involves the surgical removal of both testicles. While still a significant piece of surgery, there is not the abdominal exposure that is required in the female surgery. In addition, there is now a chemical sterilization option, in which a solution is injected into each testicle, leading to atrophy of the sperm-producing cells. This can typically be done under sedation rather than full anesthesia. This is a relatively new approach, and there are no long-term clinical studies yet available.

Neutering/spaying is typically done around six months of age at most veterinary hospitals, although techniques have been pioneered to perform the procedures in animals as young as eight weeks of age. In general, the surg-

TAKING YOUR DOG'S TEMPERATURE

It is important to know how to take your dog's temperature at times when you think he may be ill. It's not the most enjoyable task, but it can be done without too much difficulty. It's easier with a helper, preferably someone with whom the dog is friendly, so that one of you can hold the dog while the other inserts the thermometer.

Before inserting the thermometer, coat the end with petroleum jelly. Insert the thermometer slowly and gently into the dog's rectum about one inch. Wait for the reading, about two minutes. Be sure to remove the thermometer carefully and clean it thoroughly after each use.

A dog's normal body temperature is between 100.5 and 102.5 degrees F. Immediate veterinary attention is required if the dog's temperature is below 99 or above 104 degrees F.

eries on the very young animals are done for the specific reason of sterilizing them before they go to their new homes. This is done in some shelter hospitals for assurance that the animals will definitely not produce any pups. Otherwise, these organizations need to rely on owners to comply with their wishes to have the animals "altered" at a later date, something that does not always happen.

S. E. M. BY DR. DENNIS KUNKEL, UNIVERSITY OF HAWAII.

A scanning electron micrograph of a dog flea, *Ctenocephalides canis*, on dog hair.

EXTERNAL PARASITES

FLEAS

Fleas have been around for millions of years and, while we have better tools now for controlling them than at any time in the past, there still is little chance that they will end up on an endangered species list. Actually, they are very well adapted to living on our pets, and they continue to adapt as we make advances.

The female flea can consume 15 times her weight in blood during active reproduction and can lay as many as 40 eggs a day. These eggs are very resistant to the effects of insecticides. They hatch into larvae, which then mature and spin cocoons. The immature fleas reside in this pupal stage until the time is right for feeding. This pupal stage is also very resistant to the effects of insecticides, and pupae can last in the environment without feeding for many months. Newly emergent fleas are attracted to animals by the warmth of the animals' bodies, movement and exhaled carbon dioxide. However, when they first emerge from their cocoons, they orient towards light; thus when an animal passes between a flea and the light source, casting a shadow, the flea pounces and starts to feed. If the animal turns out to be a dog or cat, the reproductive cycle continues. If the flea lands on another type of animal, including a person, the flea will bite but will then look for a more appropriate host. An emerging adult flea can survive without feeding for up to 12 months but, once it tastes blood, it can survive off its host for only 3 to 4 days.

It was once thought that fleas spend most of their lives in the environment, but we now know that fleas won't willingly jump off a dog unless leaping to another dog or when physically removed by brushing, bathing or other manipulation. Flea eggs, on the other hand, are shiny and smooth, and they roll off the animal and into the environment. The eggs, larvae and pupae then exist in the environment, but once the adult finds a susceptible animal, it's home sweet home until the flea is forced to seek refuge elsewhere.

Since adult fleas live on the animal and immature forms survive in the environment, a successful treatment plan must address all stages of the flea life cycle. There are now several safe and effective flea-control products that can be applied on a monthly

> ## FLEA PREVENTION FOR YOUR DOG
> - Discuss with your veterinarian the safest product to protect your dog, likely in the form of a monthly tablet or a liquid preparation placed on the back of the dog's neck.
> - For dogs suffering from flea-bite dermatitis, a shampoo or topical insecticide treatment is required.
> - Your lawn and property should be sprayed with an insecticide designed to kill fleas and ticks that lurk outdoors.
> - Using a flea comb, check the dog's coat regularly for any signs of parasites.
> - Practice good housekeeping. Vacuum floors, carpets and furniture regularly, especially in the areas that the dog frequents, and wash the dog's bedding weekly.
> - Follow up house-cleaning with carpet shampoos and sprays to rid the house of fleas at all stages of development. Insect growth regulators are the safest option.

basis. These include fipronil, imidacloprid, selamectin and permethrin (found in several formulations). Most of these products have significant flea-killing rates within 24 hours. However, none of them will control the immature forms in the environment. To accomplish this, there are a variety of insect growth regulators that can be sprayed into

THE FLEA'S LIFE CYCLE

What came first, the flea or the egg? This age-old mystery is more difficult to comprehend than the actual cycle of the flea. Fleas usually live only about four months. A female can lay 2,000 eggs in her lifetime.

Photo by Carolina Biological Supply Co.

Egg

After ten days of rolling around your carpet or under your furniture, the eggs hatch into larvae, which feed on various and sundry debris. In days or months, depending on the climate, the larvae spin cocoons and develop into the pupal or nymph stage, which quickly develop into fleas.

Larva

Photo by Carolina Biological Supply Co.

Pupa

These immature fleas must locate a host within 10 to 14 days or they will die. Only about 1% of the flea population exist as adult fleas, while the other 99% exist as eggs, larvae or pupae.

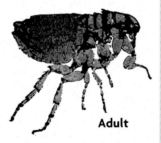

Adult

KILL FLEAS THE NATURAL WAY

If you choose not to go the route of conventional medication, there are some natural ways to ward off fleas:

- Dust your dog with a natural flea powder, composed of such herbal goodies as rosemary, wormwood, pennyroyal, citronella, rue, tobacco powder and eucalyptus.
- Apply diatomaceous earth, the fossilized remains of single-cell algae, to your carpets, furniture and pet's bedding. Even though it's not good for dogs, it's even worse for fleas, which will dry up swiftly and die.
- Brush your dog frequently, give him adequate exercise and let him fast occasionally. All of these activities strengthen the dog's immune system and make him more resistant to disease and parasites.
- Bathe your dog with a capful of pennyroyal or eucalyptus oil.
- Feed a natural diet, free of additives and preservatives. Add some fresh garlic and brewer's yeast to the dog's morning portion, as these items have flea-repelling properties.

the environment (e.g., pyriproxyfen, methoprene, fenoxycarb) as well as insect development inhibitors such as lufenuron that can be administered. These compounds have no effect on adult fleas, but they stop immature forms from developing into

adults. In years gone by, we relied heavily on toxic insecticides (such as organophosphates, organochlorines and carbamates) to manage the flea problem, but today's options are not only much safer to use on our pets but also safer for the environment.

Ticks

Ticks are members of the spider class (arachnids) and are blood-sucking parasites capable of transmitting a variety of diseases, including Lyme disease, ehrlichiosis, babesiosis and Rocky Mountain spotted fever. It's easy to see ticks on your own skin, but it is more of a challenge when your furry companion is affected. Whenever you happen to be planning a stroll in a tick-infested area (especially forests, grassy or wooded areas or parks) be prepared to do a thorough inspection of your dog afterward to search for ticks. Ticks can be tricky, so make sure you spend time looking in the ears, between the toes and everywhere else where a tick might hide. Ticks need to be attached for 24–72 hours before they transmit most of the diseases that they carry, so you do have a window of opportunity for some preventive intervention.

A TICKING BOMB

There is nothing good about a tick's harpooning his nose into your dog's skin. Among the diseases caused by ticks are Rocky Mountain spotted fever, canine ehrlichiosis, canine babesiosis, canine hepatozoonosis and Lyme disease. If a dog is allergic to the saliva of a female wood tick, he can develop tick paralysis.

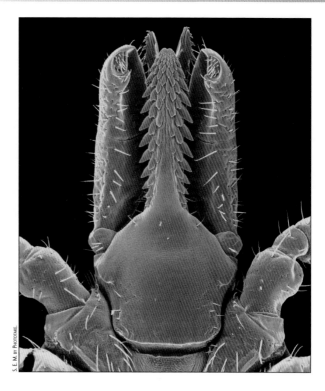

S. E. M. BY PHOTOTAKE.

Female ticks live to eat and breed. They can lay between 4,000 and 5,000 eggs and they die soon after. Males, on the other hand, live only to mate with the females and continue the process as long as they are able. Most ticks live on multiple hosts before parasitizing dogs. The immature forms typically reside on grass and shrubs, waiting for susceptible animals to walk by. The larvae and nymph stages typically feed on wildlife.

If only a few ticks are present on a dog, they can be plucked out, but it is important to remove the entire head and mouthparts,

A scanning electron micrograph of the head of a female deer tick, *Ixodes dammini*, a parasitic tick that carries Lyme disease.

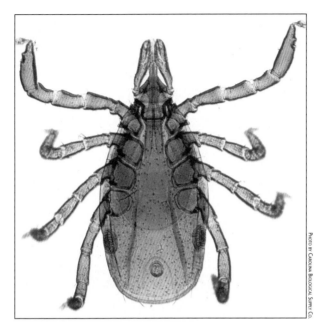

**Deer tick,
Ixodes dammini.**

PHOTO BY CAROLINA BIOLOGICAL SUPPLY CO.

which may be deeply embedded in the skin. This is best accomplished with forceps designed especially for this purpose; fingers can be used but should be protected with rubber gloves, plastic wrap or at least a paper towel. The tick should be grasped as closely as possible to the animal's skin and should be pulled upward with steady, even pressure. Do not squeeze, crush or puncture the body of the tick or you risk exposure to any disease carried by that tick. Once the ticks have been removed, the sites of attachment should be disinfected. Your hands should then be washed with soap and water to further minimize risk of contagion. The tick should be disposed of in a container of alcohol or household bleach.

Some of the newer flea products, specifically those with fipronil, selamectin and permethrin, have effect against some, but not all, species of tick. Flea collars containing appropriate pesticides (e.g., propoxur, chlorfenvinphos) can aid in tick control. In most areas, such collars should be placed on animals in March, at the beginning of the tick season, and changed regularly. Leaving the collar on when the pesticide level is waning invites the development of resistance. Amitraz collars are also good for tick control, and the active ingredient does not interfere with other flea-control products. The ingredient helps prevent the attachment of ticks to the skin and will cause those ticks already on the skin to detach themselves.

TICK CONTROL

Removal of underbrush and leaf litter and the thinning of trees in areas where tick control is desired are recommended. These actions remove the cover and food sources for small animals that serve as hosts for ticks. With continued mowing of grasses in these areas, the probability of ticks' surviving is further reduced. A variety of insecticide ingredients (e.g., resmethrin, carbaryl, permethrin, chlorpyrifos, dioxathion and allethrin) are registered for tick control around the home.

MITES

Mites are tiny arachnid parasites that parasitize the skin of dogs. Skin diseases caused by mites are referred to as "mange," and there are many different forms seen in dogs. These forms are very different from one another, each one warranting an individual description.

Sarcoptic mange, or scabies, is one of the itchiest conditions that affects dogs. The microscopic *Sarcoptes* mites burrow into the superficial layers of the skin and can drive dogs crazy with itchiness. They are also communicable to people, although they can't complete their reproductive cycle on people. In addition to being tiny, the mites also are often difficult to find when trying to make a diagnosis. Skin scrapings from multiple areas are examined microscopically but, even then, sometimes the mites cannot be found.

Fortunately, scabies is relatively easy to treat, and there are a variety of products that will successfully kill the mites. Since the mites can't live in the environment for very long without feeding, a complete cure is usually possible within four to eight weeks.

Cheyletiellosis is caused by a relatively large mite, which sometimes can be seen even without a microscope. Often referred to as "walking dandruff," this also causes itching, but not usually as profound as with scabies. While *Cheyletiella* mites can survive somewhat longer

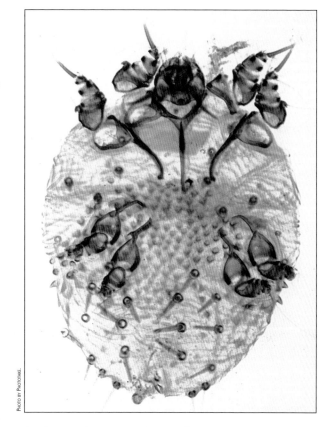

PHOTO BY PHOTOTAKE.

Sarcoptes scabiei, commonly known as the "itch mite."

in the environment than scabies mites, they too are relatively easy to treat, being responsive to not only the medications used to treat scabies but also often to flea-control products.

Otodectes cynotis is the canine ear mite and is one of the more common causes of mange, especially in young dogs in shelters or pet stores. That's because the mites are typically present in large numbers and are quickly spread to nearby animals. The mites rarely do much harm but

Micrograph of a dog louse, *Heterodoxus spiniger*. Female lice attach their eggs to the hairs of the dog. As the eggs hatch, the larval lice bite and feed on the blood. Lice can also feed on dead skin and hair. This feeding activity can cause hair loss and skin problems.

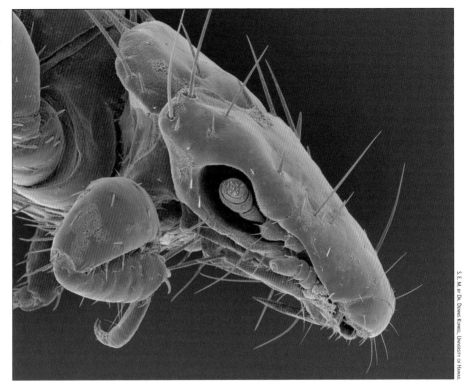

S. E. M. BY DR. DENNIS KUNKEL, UNIVERSITY OF HAWAII.

can be difficult to eradicate if the treatment regimen is not comprehensive. While many try to treat the condition with ear drops only, this is the most common cause of treatment failure. Ear drops cause the mites to simply move out of the ears and as far away as possible (usually to the base of the tail) until the insecticide levels in the ears drop to an acceptable level—then it's back to business as usual! The successful treatment of ear mites requires treating all animals in the household with a systemic insecticide, such as selamectin, or a combination of miticidal ear

drops combined with whole-body flea-control preparations.

Demodicosis, sometimes referred to as red mange, can be one of the most difficult forms of mange to treat. Part of the problem has to do with the fact that the mites live in the hair follicles and they are relatively well shielded from topical and systemic products. The main issue, however, is that demodectic mange typically results only when there is some underlying process interfering with the dog's immune system.

Since *Demodex* mites are normal residents of the skin of

mammals, including humans, there is usually a mite population explosion only when the immune system fails to keep the number of mites in check. In young animals, the immune deficit may be transient or may reflect an actual inherited immune problem. In older animals, demodicosis is usually seen only when there is another disease hampering the immune system, such as diabetes, cancer, thyroid problems or the use of immune-suppressing drugs. Accordingly, treatment involves not only trying to kill the mange mites but also discerning what is interfering with immune function and correcting it if possible.

Chiggers represent several different species of mite that don't parasitize dogs specifically, but do latch on to passersby and can cause irritation. The problem is most prevalent in wooded areas in the late summer and fall. Treatment is not difficult, as the mites do not complete their life cycle on dogs and are susceptible to a variety of miticidal products.

MOSQUITOES

Mosquitoes have long been known to transmit a variety of diseases to people, as well as just being biting pests during warm weather. They also pose a real risk to pets. Not only do they carry deadly heartworms but

recently there also has been much concern over their involvement with West Nile virus. While we can avoid heartworm with the use of preventive medications, there are no such preventives for West Nile virus. The only method of prevention in endemic areas is active mosquito control. Fortunately, most dogs that have been exposed to the virus only developed flu-like symptoms and, to date, there have not been the large number of reported deaths in canines as seen in some other species.

Illustration of *Demodex folliculoram.*

MOSQUITO REPELLENT

Low concentrations of DEET (less than 10%), found in many human mosquito repellents, have been safely used on dogs but, in these concentrations, probably give only about two hours of protection. DEET may be safe in these small concentrations, but since it is not licensed for use on dogs, there is no research proving its safety for dogs. Products containing permethrin give the longest-lasting protection, perhaps two to four weeks. As DEET is not licensed for use on dogs, and both DEET and permethrin can be quite toxic to cats, appropriate care should be exercised. Other products, such as those containing oil of citronella, also have some mosquito-repellent activity, but typically have a relatively short duration of action.

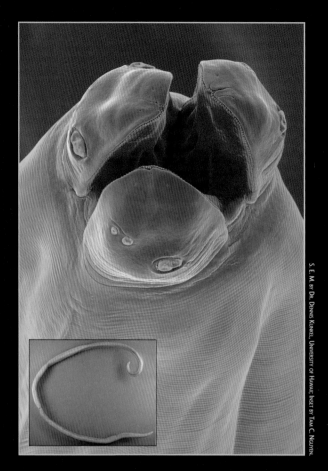

S. E. M. BY DR. DENNIS KUNKEL, UNIVERSITY OF HAWAII; INSET BY TAM C. NGUYEN.

ASCARID DANGERS

The most commonly encountered worms in dogs are roundworms known as ascarids. *Toxascaris leonine* and *Toxocara canis* are the two species that infect dogs. Subsisting in the dog's stomach and intestines, adult round-worms can grow to 7 inches in length and adult females can lay in excess of 200,000 eggs in a single day.

In humans, visceral larval migrans affects people who have ingested eggs of *Toxocara canis*, which frequently contaminates children's sandboxes, beaches and park grounds. The round-worms reside in the human's stomach and intestines, as they would in a dog's, but do not mature. Instead, they find their way to the liver, lungs and skin, or even to the heart or kidneys in severe cases. Deworming puppies is critical in preventing the infection in humans, and young children should never handle nursing pups who have not been dewormed.

The ascarid roundworm *Toxocara canis*, showing the mouth with three lips. INSET: Photomicrograph of the roundworm *Ascaris lumbricoides.*

INTERNAL PARASITES: WORMS

ASCARIDS

Ascarids are intestinal round-worms that rarely cause severe disease in dogs. Nonetheless, they are of major public health signifi-cance because they can be trans-ferred to people. Sadly, it is chil-dren who are most commonly affected by the parasite, probably from inadvertently ingesting ascarid-contaminated soil. In fact, many yards and children's sand-boxes contain appreciable numbers of ascarid eggs. So, while ascarids don't bite dogs or latch onto their intestines to suck blood, they do cause some nasty medical conditions in children and are best eradicated from our furry friends. Because pups can start passing ascarid eggs by three weeks of age, most parasite-control programs begin at two weeks of age and are repeated every two weeks until pups are eight weeks old. It is important to

HOOKED ON ANCYLOSTOMA

Adult dogs can become infected by the bloodsucking nematodes we commonly call hookworms via ingesting larvae from the ground or via the larvae penetrating the dog's skin. It is not uncommon for infected dogs to show no symptoms of hookworm infestation. Sometimes symptoms occur within ten days of exposure. These symptoms can include bloody diarrhea, anemia, loss of weight and general weakness. Dogs pass the hookworm eggs in their stools, which serves as the vet's method of identifying the infestation. The hookworm larvae can encyst themselves in the dog's tissues and be released when the dog is experiencing stress.

Caused by an *Ancylostoma* species whose common host is the dog, cutaneous larval migrans affects humans, causing itching and lumps and streaks beneath the surface of the skin.

S. E. M. BY DR. DENNIS KUNKEL, UNIVERSITY OF HAWAII.

realize that bitches can pass ascarids to their pups even if they test negative prior to whelping. Accordingly, bitches are best treated at the same time as the pups.

HOOKWORMS
Unlike ascarids, hookworms do latch onto a dog's intestinal tract and can cause significant loss of blood and protein. Similar to ascarids, hookworms can be transmitted to humans, where they cause a condition known as cutaneous larval migrans. Dogs can become infected either by consuming the infective larvae or by the larvae's penetrating the skin directly. People most often get infected when they are lying on the ground (such as on a beach) and the larvae penetrate the skin. Yes, the larvae can penetrate through a beach blanket. Hookworms are typically susceptible to the same medications used to treat ascarids.

The hookworm *Ancylostoma caninum* infests the intestines of dogs. INSET: Note the row of hooks at the posterior end, used to anchor the worm to the intestinal wall.

WHIPWORMS

Whipworms latch onto the lower aspects of the dog's colon and can cause cramping and diarrhea. Eggs do not start to appear in the dog's feces until about three months after the dog was infected. This worm has a peculiar life cycle, which makes it more difficult to control than ascarids or hook-worms. The good thing is that whipworms rarely are transferred to people.

Some of the medications used to treat ascarids and hookworms are also effective against whipworms, but, in general, a separate treatment protocol is needed. Since most of the medications are effective against the adults but not the eggs or larvae, treatment is typically repeated in three weeks, and then often in three

Adult whipworm, *Trichuris* sp., an intestinal parasite.

S. E. M. BY DR. DENNIS KUNKEL, UNIVERSITY OF HAWAII.

WORM-CONTROL GUIDELINES

- Practice sanitary habits with your dog and home.
- Clean up after your dog and don't let him sniff or eat other dogs' droppings.
- Control insects and fleas in the dog's environment. Fleas, lice, cockroaches, beetles, mice and rats can act as hosts for various worms.
- Prevent dogs from eating uncooked meat, raw poultry and dead animals.
- Keep dogs and children from playing in sand and soil.
- Kennel dogs on cement or gravel; avoid dirt runs.
- Administer heartworm preventives regularly.
- Have your vet examine your dog's stools at your annual visits.
- Select a boarding kennel carefully so as to avoid contamination from other dogs or an unsanitary environment.
- Prevent dogs from roaming. Obey local leash laws.

months as well. Unfortunately, since dogs don't develop resistance to whipworms, it is difficult to prevent them from getting rein-fected if they visit soil contami-nated with whipworm eggs.

TAPEWORMS

There are many different species of tapeworm that affect dogs, but *Dipylidium caninum* is probably the most common and is spread by fleas. Flea larvae feed on organic debris and tapeworm eggs in the environment and, when a dog chews at himself and manages to ingest fleas, he might get a dose of tapeworm at the same time. The tapeworm then develops further in the intestine of the dog.

The tapeworm itself, which is a parasitic flatworm that latches onto the intestinal wall, is composed of numerous segments. When the segments break off into the intestine (as proglottids), they may accumulate around the rectum, like grains of rice. While this tapeworm is disgusting in its behavior, it is not directly communicable to humans (although humans can also get infected by swallowing fleas).

A much more dangerous flatworm is *Echinococcus multilocularis*, which is typically found in foxes, coyotes and wolves. The eggs are passed in the feces and infect rodents, and, when dogs eat the rodents, the dogs can be infected by thousands of adult tapeworms. While the parasites don't cause many problems in dogs, this is considered the most lethal worm infection that people can get. Take appropriate precautions if you live in an area in which these tapeworms are found. Do not use mulch that may contain feces of dogs, cats or wildlife, and discourage your pets from hunting

wildlife. Treat these tapeworm infections aggressively in pets, because if humans get infected, approximately half die.

HEARTWORMS

Heartworm disease is caused by the parasite *Dirofilaria immitis* and is seen in dogs around the world. A member of the roundworm group, it is spread between dogs by the bite of an infected mosquito. The mosquito injects infective larvae into the dog's skin with its bite, and these larvae develop under the skin for a period of time before making their way to the heart. There they develop into adults, which grow and create blockages of the heart, lungs and major blood vessels there. They also start producing offspring (microfilariae),

A dog tapeworm proglottid (body segment).

The dog tapeworm *Taenia pisiformis*.

A Look at Internal Parasites

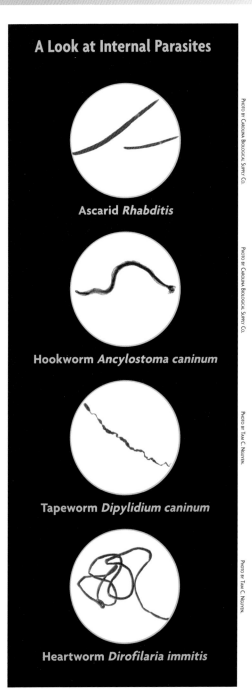

Ascarid *Rhabditis*

Hookworm *Ancylostoma caninum*

Tapeworm *Dipylidium caninum*

Heartworm *Dirofilaria immitis*

PHOTO BY CAROLINA BIOLOGICAL SUPPLY CO.

PHOTO BY CAROLINA BIOLOGICAL SUPPLY CO.

PHOTO BY TAM C. NGUYEN.

PHOTO BY TAM C. NGUYEN.

and these microfilariae circulate in the bloodstream, waiting to hitch a ride when the next mosquito bites. Once in the mosquito, the microfilariae develop into infective larvae and the entire process is repeated.

When dogs get infected with heartworm, over time they tend to develop symptoms associated with heart disease, such as coughing, exercise intolerance and potentially many other manifestations. Diagnosis is confirmed by either seeing the microfilariae themselves in blood samples or using immunologic tests (antigen testing) to identify the presence of adult heartworms. Since antigen tests measure the presence of adult heartworms and microfilarial tests measure offspring produced by adults, neither are positive until six to seven months after the initial infection. However, the beginning of damage can occur by fifth-stage larvae as early as three months after infection. Thus it is possible for dogs to be harboring problem-causing larvae for up to three months before either type of test would identify an infection.

The good news is that there are great protocols available for preventing heartworm in dogs. Testing is critical in the process, and it is important to understand the benefits as well as the limitations of such testing. All dogs six months of age or older that have not been on continuous heartworm-preventive medication

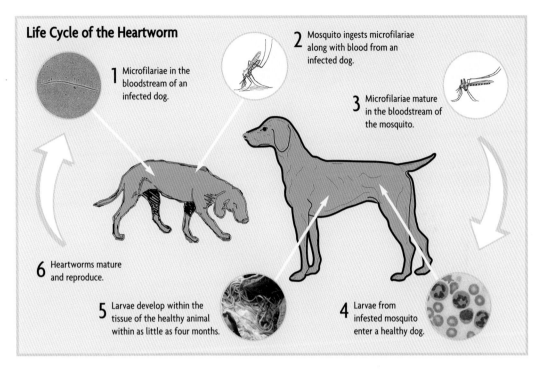

Life Cycle of the Heartworm

1 Microfilariae in the bloodstream of an infected dog.

2 Mosquito ingests microfilariae along with blood from an infected dog.

3 Microfilariae mature in the bloodstream of the mosquito.

4 Larvae from infested mosquito enter a healthy dog.

5 Larvae develop within the tissue of the healthy animal within as little as four months.

6 Heartworms mature and reproduce.

should be screened with microfilarial or antigen tests. For dogs receiving preventive medication, periodic antigen testing helps assess the effectiveness of the preventives. The American Heartworm Society guidelines suggest that annual retesting may not be necessary when owners have absolutely provided continuous heartworm prevention. Retesting on a two- to three-year interval may be sufficient in these cases. However, your veterinarian will likely have specific guidelines under which heartworm preventives will be prescribed, and many prefer to err on the side of safety and retest annually.

It is indeed fortunate that heartworm is relatively easy to prevent, because treatments can be as life-threatening as the disease itself. Treatment requires a two-step process that kills the adult heartworms first and then the microfilariae. Prevention is obviously preferable; this involves a once-monthly oral or topical treatment. The most common oral preventives include ivermectin (not suitable for some breeds), moxidectin and milbemycin oxime; the once-a-month topical drug selamectin provides heartworm protection in addition to flea, some type of tick and other parasite controls.

THE **ABC**s OF
Emergency Care

Abrasions
Clean wound with running water or 3% hydrogen peroxide. Pat dry with gauze and spray with antibiotic. Do not cover.

Animal Bites
Clean area with soap and saline solution or water. Apply pressure to any bleeding area. Apply antibiotic ointment. Identify biting animal and contact the vet.

Antifreeze Poisoning
Induce vomiting and take dog to the vet.

Bee Sting
Remove stinger and apply soothing lotion or cold compress; give antihistamine in proper dosage.

Bleeding
Apply pressure directly to wound with gauze or towel for five to ten minutes. If wound does not stop bleeding, wrap wound with gauze and adhesive tape.

Bloat/Gastric Torsion
Immediately take the dog to the vet or emergency clinic; phone from car. No time to waste.

Burns
Chemical: Bathe dog with water and pet shampoo. Rinse in saline solution. Apply antibiotic ointment.

Acid: Rinse with water. Apply one part baking soda, two parts water to affected area.

Alkali: Rinse with water. Apply one part vinegar, four parts water to affected area.

Electrical: Apply antibiotic ointment. Seek veterinary assistance immediately.

Choking
If the dog is on the verge of collapsing, wedge a solid object, such as the handle of a screwdriver, between molars on one side of mouth to keep mouth open. Pull tongue out. Use long-nosed pliers or fingers to remove foreign object. Do not push the object down the dog's throat. For small or medium dogs, hold dog upside down by hind legs and shake firmly to dislodge foreign object.

Chlorine Ingestion
With clean water, rinse the mouth and eyes. Give dog water to drink; contact the vet.

Constipation
Feed dog 2 tablespoons bran flakes with each meal. Encourage drinking water. Mix 1/4-teaspoon mineral oil in dog's food. Contact vet if persists longer than 24 hours.

Diarrhea
Withhold food for 12 to 24 hours. Feed dog anti-diarrheal with eyedropper. When feeding resumes, feed one part boiled hamburger, one part plain cooked rice, 1/4 to 3/4 cup four times daily. Contact vet if persists longer than 24 hours.

Dog Bite
Snip away hair around puncture wound; clean with 3% hydrogen peroxide; apply tincture of iodine. Identify biting dog and call the vet. If wound appears deep, take the dog to the vet.

Frostbite
Wrap the dog in a heavy blanket. Warm affected area with a warm bath for ten minutes. Red color to skin will return with circulation; if tissues are pale after 20 minutes, contact the vet.

Use a portable, durable container large enough to contain all items.

Heat Stroke
Submerge the dog (up to his muzzle) in cold water; if no response within ten minutes, contact the vet.

Hot Spots
Mix 2 packets Domeboro® with 2 cups water. Saturate cloth with mixture and apply to hot spots for 15–30 minutes. Apply antibiotic ointment. Repeat every six to eight hours.

Poisonous Plants
Wash affected area with soap and water. Cleanse with alcohol. For foxtail/grass, apply antibiotic ointment. Contact vet if plant was ingested.

Rat Poison Ingestion
Induce vomiting. Keep dog calm, maintain dog's normal body temperature (use blanket or heating pad). Get to the vet for antidote.

Shock
Keep the dog calm and warm; call for veterinary assistance.

Snake Bite
If possible, bandage the area and apply pressure. If the area is not conducive to bandaging, use ice to control bleeding. Get immediate help from the vet.

Tick Removal
Apply flea and tick spray directly on tick. Wait one minute. Using tweezers or wearing plastic gloves, grasp the tick's body firmly. Apply antibiotic ointment.

Vomiting
Restrict water intake; offer a few ice cubes. Withhold food for next meal. Contact vet if vomiting persists longer than 24 hours.

DOG OWNER'S FIRST-AID KIT
- ☐ Gauze bandages/swabs
- ☐ Adhesive and non-adhesive bandages
- ☐ Antibiotic powder
- ☐ Antiseptic wash
- ☐ Hydrogen peroxide 3%
- ☐ Antibiotic ointment
- ☐ Lubricating jelly
- ☐ Rectal thermometer
- ☐ Nylon muzzle
- ☐ Scissors and forceps
- ☐ Eyedropper
- ☐ Syringe
- ☐ Anti-bacterial/fungal solution
- ☐ Saline solution
- ☐ Antihistamine
- ☐ Cotton balls
- ☐ Nail clippers
- ☐ Screwdriver/pen knife
- ☐ Flashlight
- ☐ Emergency phone numbers

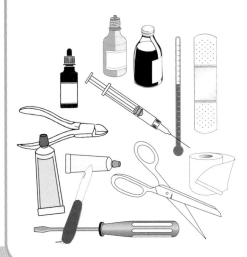

A Puli should have clear, healthy eyes.

A PET OWNER'S GUIDE TO COMMON OPHTHALMIC DISEASES
by Prof. Dr. Robert L. Peiffer, Jr.

Few would argue that vision is the most important of the cognitive senses, and maintenance of a normal visual system is important for an optimal quality of life. Likewise, pet owners tend to be acutely aware of their pet's eyes and vision, which is important because early detection of ocular disease will optimize therapeutic outcomes. The eye is a sensitive organ with minimal reparative capabilities, and with some diseases, such as glaucoma, uveitis and retinal detachment, early diagnosis and treatment can be critical in terms of whether vision can be preserved.

The causes of ocular disease are quite varied; the nature of dogs makes them susceptible to traumatic conditions, the most common of which include proptosis of the globe, cat scratch injuries and penetrating wounds

Lower entropion, or rolling in of the eyelid, is causing irritation in the left eye of this young dog. Several extra eyelashes, a condition called distichiasis, are present on the upper lid.

from foreign objects, including sticks and air rifle pellets. Infectious diseases caused by bacteria, viruses or fungi may be localized to the eye or part of a systemic infection. Many of the common conditions, including eyelid conformational problems, cataracts, glaucoma and retinal degenerations have a genetic basis.

Before acquiring your puppy it is important to ascertain that both parents have been examined and certified as free of eye disease by a veterinary ophthalmologist. Since many of these genetic diseases can be detected early in life, acquire the pup on the condition that he pass a thorough ophthalmic examination by a qualified specialist.

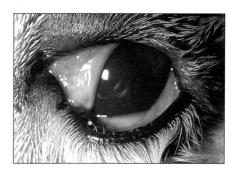

LID CONFORMATIONAL ABNORMALITIES
Rolling in (entropion) or out (ectropion) of the lids tends to be a breed-related problem. Entropion can involve the upper and/or lower lids. Signs usually appear between 3 and 12 months of age. The irritation caused by the eyelid

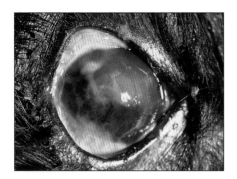

hairs' rubbing on the surface of the cornea may result in blinking, tearing and damage to the cornea. Ectropion is likewise breed-related and is considered "normal" in hounds, for instance; unlike entropion, which results in acute discomfort, ectropion may cause chronic irritation related to exposure and the pooling of secretions. Most of these cases can be managed medically with daily irrigation with sterile saline and topical antibiotics when required.

EYELASH ABNORMALITIES
Dogs normally have lashes only on the upper lids, in contrast to humans. Occasionally extra eyelashes may be seen emerging

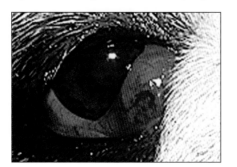

at the eyelid margin (distichiasis) or through the inner surface of the eyelid (ectopic cilia).

CONJUNCTIVITIS
Inflammation of the conjunctiva, the pink tissue that lines the lids and the anterior portion of the sclera, is generally accompanied by redness, discharge and mild discomfort. The majority of cases are associated with either bacterial infections or dry eye syndrome. Fortunately, topical medications are generally effective in curing or controlling the problem.

DRY EYE SYNDROME
Dry eye syndrome (keratoconjunctivitis sicca) is a common cause of external ocular disease. Discharge is typically thick and sticky, and keratitis is a frequent component; any breed can be affected. While some cases can be associated with toxic effects of drugs, including the sulfa antibiotics, the cause in the majority of the cases cannot be determined and is assumed to be immune-mediated.

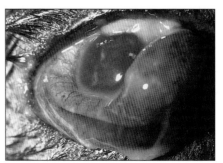

Keratoconjunctivitis sicca, seen here in the right eye of a middle-aged dog, causes a characteristic thick mucus discharge as well as secondary corneal changes.

LEFT: Prolapse of the gland of the third eyelid in the right eye of a pup. RIGHT: In this case, in the right eye of a young dog, the prolapsed gland can be seen emerging between the edge of the third eyelid and the corneal surface.

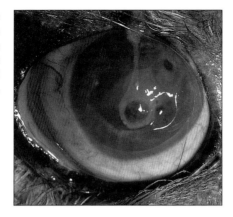

Multiple deep ulcerations affect the cornea of this middle-aged dog.

PROLAPSE OF THE GLAND OF THE THIRD EYELID

In this condition, commonly referred to as *cherry eye*, the gland of the third eyelid, which produces about one-third of the aqueous phase of the tear film and is normally situated within the anterior orbit, prolapses to emerge as a pink fleshy mass protruding over the edge of the third eyelid, between the third eyelid and the cornea. The condition usually develops during the first year of life and, while mild irritation may result, the condition is unsightly as much as anything else.

CORNEAL DISEASE

The cornea is the clear front part of the eye that provides the first step in the collection of light on its journey to be eventually focused onto the retina, and most corneal diseases will be manifested by alterations in corneal transparency. The cornea is an exquisitely innervated tissue, and

Lipid deposition can occur as a primary inherited dystrophy, or secondarily to hypercholesterolemia (in dogs frequently associated with hypothyroidism), chronic corneal inflammation or neoplasia. The deposits in this dog assume an oval pattern in the center of the cornea.

defects in corneal integrity are accompanied by pain, which is demonstrated by squinting.

Corneal ulcers may occur secondarily to trauma or to irritation from entropion or ectopic cilia. In middle-aged or older dogs, epithelial ulcerations may occur spontaneously due to an inherent defect; these are referred to as indolent or Boxer ulcers, in recognition of the breed in which we see the condition most frequently. Infection may occur secondarily. Ulcers can be potentially blinding conditions; severity is dependent upon the size and depth of the ulcer and other complicating features.

Non-ulcerative keratitis tends to have an immune-mediated component and is managed by topical immunosuppressants, usually corticosteroids. Corneal edema can occur in elderly dogs. It is due to a failure of the corneal endothelial "pump."

The cornea responds to chronic irritation by transforming into skin-like tissue that is

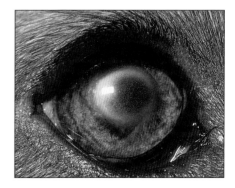

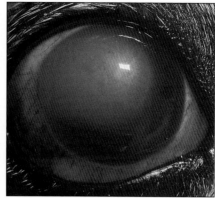

evident clinically by pigmentation, scarring and vascularization; some cases may respond to tear stimulants, lubricants and topical corticosteroids, while others benefit from surgical narrowing of the eyelid opening in order to enhance corneal protection.

UVEITIS

Inflammation of the vascular tissue of the eye—the uvea—is a common and potentially serious disease in dogs. While it may occur secondarily to trauma or other intraocular diseases, such as cataracts, most commonly uveitis

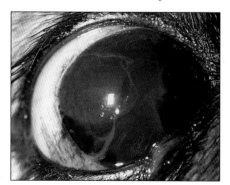

is associated with some type of systemic infectious or neoplastic process. Uncontrolled, uveitis can lead to blinding cataracts, glaucoma and/or retinal detachments, and aggressive symptomatic therapy with dilating agents (to prevent pupillary adhesions) and anti-inflammatories is critical.

GLAUCOMA

The eye is essentially a hollow fluid-filled sphere, and the pressure within is maintained by regulation of the rate of fluid production and fluid egress at 10–20 mm of mercury. The retinal cells are extremely sensitive to elevations of intraocular pressure and, unless controlled, permanent blindness can occur within hours to days. In acute glaucoma, the conjunctiva becomes congested, the cornea cloudy, the pupil moderate and fixed; the eye is generally painful and avisual. Increased constant signs of discomfort will accompany chronic cases.

Corneal edema can develop as a slowly progressive process in elderly Boston Terriers, Miniature Dachshunds and Miniature Poodles, as well as others, as a result of the inability of the corneal endothelial "pump" to maintain a state of dehydration.

Medial pigmentary keratitis in this dog is associated with irritation from prominent facial folds.

Glaucoma in the dog most commonly occurs as a sudden extreme elevation of intraocular pressure, frequently to three to four times the norm. The eye of this dog demonstrates the common signs of episcleral injection, or redness; mild diffuse corneal cloudiness, due to edema; and a mid-sized fixed pupil.

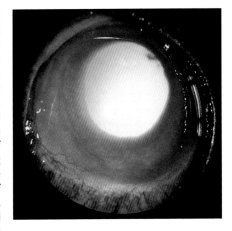

Management of glaucoma is one of the most challenging situations that the veterinary ophthalmologist faces; in spite of intense efforts, many of these cases will result in blindness.

CATARACTS AND LENS DISLOCATION
Cataracts are the most common blinding condition in dogs; fortunately, they are readily amenable to surgical intervention, with excellent results in terms of restoration of vision and replacement of the cataractous lens with a synthetic one. Most cataracts in

dogs are inherited; less commonly cataracts can be secondary to trauma or other ocular diseases, including uveitis, glaucoma, lens luxation and retinal degeneration, or secondary to an underlying systemic metabolic disease, including diabetes and Cushing's disease. Signs include a progressive loss of the bright dark appearance of the pupil, which is replaced by a blue-gray hazy appearance. In this respect, cataracts need to be distinguished from the normal aging process of nuclear sclerosis, which occurs in middle-aged or older animals, and has minimal effect on vision.

Lens dislocation occurs in dogs and frequently leads to secondary glaucoma; early removal of the dislocated lens is generally curative.

RETINAL DISEASE
Retinal degenerations are usually inherited but may be associated with vitamin E deficiency in dogs. While signs are variable,

LEFT: The typical posterior subcapsular cataract appears between one and two years of age, but rarely progresses to where the animal has visual problems. RIGHT: Inherited cataracts generally appear between three and six years of age, and progress to the stage seen where functional vision is significantly impaired.

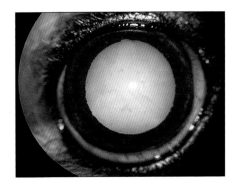

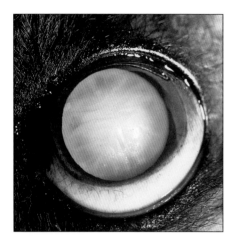

most frequently one notes a decrease in vision over a period of months, which typically starts out as a night blindness. The cause of a more rapid loss of vision due to retinal degeneration occurs over days to weeks and is labeled sudden acquired retinal degeneration or SARD; the outcome, however, is unfortunately usually similar to inherited and nutritional conditions,

as the retinal tissues possess minimal regenerative capabilities. Most pets, however, with a bit of extra care and attention, show an amazing ability to adapt to an avisual world, and can be maintained as pets with a satisfactory quality of life.

Detachment of the retina—due to accumulation of blood between the retina and the underlying uvea, which is called the *choroid*—can occur secondarily to retinal tears or holes or to tractional forces within the eye, or as a result of uveitis. These types of detachments may be amenable to surgical repair if diagnosed early.

OPTIC NEURITIS
Optic neuritis, or inflammation of the nerve that connects the eye with the brain stem, is a relatively uncommon condition that occurs usually with rather sudden loss of vision and widely dilated non-responsive pupils.

Anterior lens luxation can occur as a primary disease in the terrier breeds, or secondarily to trauma. The fibers that hold the lens in place rupture and the lens may migrate through the pupil to be situated in front of the iris. Secondary glaucoma is a frequent and significant complication that can be avoided if the dislocated lens is removed surgically.

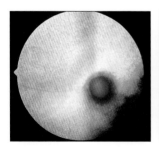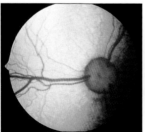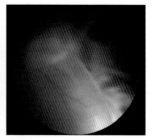

LEFT: The posterior pole of a normal fundus is shown; prominent are the head of the optic nerve and the retinal blood vessels. The retina is transparent, and the prominent green tapetum is seen superiorly.
CENTER: An eye with inherited retinal dysplasia is depicted. The tapetal retina superior to the optic disc is disorganized, with multifocal areas of hyperplasia of the retinal pigment epithelium.
RIGHT: Severe collie eye anomaly and a retinal detachment; this eye is unfortunately blind.

Number-One Killer Disease in Dogs: CANCER

In every age, there is a word associated with a disease or plague that causes humans to shudder. In the 21st century, that word is "cancer." Just as cancer is the leading cause of death in humans, it claims nearly half the lives of dogs that die from a natural disease as well as half the dogs that die over the age of ten years.

Described as a genetic disease, cancer becomes a greater risk as the dog ages. Vets and dog owners have become increasingly aware of the threat of cancer to dogs. Statistics reveal that one dog in every five will develop cancer, the most common of which is skin cancer. Many cancers, including prostate, ovarian and breast cancer, can be avoided by spaying and neutering our dogs by the age of six months.

Early detection of cancer can save or extend a dog's life, so it is absolutely vital for owners to have their dogs examined by a qualified vet or oncologist immediately upon detection of any abnormality. Certain dietary guidelines have also proven to reduce the onset and spread of cancer. Foods based on fish rather than beef, due to the presence of Omega-3 fatty acids, are recommended. Other amino acids such as glutamine have significant benefits for canines, particularly those breeds that show a greater susceptibility to cancer.

Cancer management and treatments promise hope for future generations of canines. Since the disease is genetic, breeders should never breed a dog whose parents, grandparents and any related siblings have developed cancer. It is difficult to know whether to exclude an otherwise healthy dog from a breeding program, as the disease does not manifest itself until the dog's senior years.

RECOGNIZE CANCER WARNING SIGNS

Since early detection can possibly rescue your dog from becoming a cancer statistic, it is essential for owners to recognize the possible signs and seek the assistance of a qualified professional.

- Abnormal bumps or lumps that continue to grow
- Bleeding or discharge from any body cavity
- Persistent stiffness or lameness
- Recurrent sores or sores that do not heal
- Inappetence
- Breathing difficulties
- Weight loss
- Bad breath or odors
- General malaise and fatigue
- Eating and swallowing problems
- Difficulty urinating and defecating

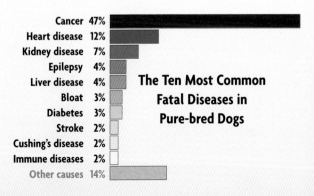

Cancer	47%
Heart disease	12%
Kidney disease	7%
Epilepsy	4%
Liver disease	4%
Bloat	3%
Diabetes	3%
Stroke	2%
Cushing's disease	2%
Immune diseases	2%
Other causes	14%

The Ten Most Common Fatal Diseases in Pure-bred Dogs

CANINE COGNITIVE DYSFUNCTION

"OLD-DOG SYNDROME"

There are many ways for you to evaluate old-dog syndrome. Veterinarians have defined canine cognitive dysfunction as the gradual deterioration of cognitive abilities, indicated by changes in the dog's behavior. When a dog changes his routine response, and maladies have been eliminated as the cause of these behavioral changes, then canine cognitive dysfunction is the usual diagnosis.

More than half the dogs over eight years old suffer from some form of cognitive dysfunction. The older the dog, the more chance he has of suffering from cognitive dysfunction. In humans, doctors often dismiss the cognitive-dysfunction behavioral changes as part of "winding down."

There are four major signs of canine cognitive dysfunction: frequent potty accidents inside the home, sleeping much more or much less than normal, acting confused and failing to respond to social stimuli. There are medications available to help affected dogs.

SYMPTOMS OF CANINE COGNITIVE DYSFUNCTION

FREQUENT POTTY ACCIDENTS
- Urinates in the house.
- Defecates in the house.
- Doesn't signal that he wants to go out.

FAILURE TO RESPOND TO SOCIAL STIMULI
- Comes to people less frequently, whether called or not.
- Doesn't tolerate petting for more than a short time.
- Doesn't come to the door when you return home.

CONFUSION
- Goes outside and just stands there.
- Appears confused with a faraway look in his eyes.
- Hides more often.
- Doesn't recognize friends.
- Doesn't come when called.
- Walks around listlessly and without a destination.

SLEEP PATTERNS
- Awakens more slowly.
- Sleeps more than normal during the day.
- Sleeps less during the night.

PULI

The Puli is well known for its longevity, and dogs living into their mid-teens are quite normal in the breed. Providing a sensible diet and exercise routine ensures that your Puli will enjoy the longevity of his forefathers. If dogs are over-indulged and allowed to become obese, they will in turn become reluctant to take exercise, which ultimately can shorten their lifespan. We have been fortunate, having had senior dogs (over seven years of age) who behave and look like youngsters. Few breeds compare to the longevity of the Puli, save those long-lived tykes in the Toy Group!

When we bring home a puppy, full of the energy and exuberance that accompanies youth, we hope for a long, happy and fulfilling relationship with the new family member. Even when we adopt an older dog, we look forward to the years of companionship ahead with a new canine friend. However, aging is inevitable for all creatures, and there will come a time when your Puli reaches his senior years and will need special considerations and attention to his care.

WHEN IS MY DOG A "SENIOR"?
In general, pure-bred dogs are considered to have achieved senior status when they reach 75% of their breed's average lifespan, with lifespan being based on breed size. Your Puli has an average lifespan of 10–15 and thus is considered a senior citizen at around 7 or 8.

Obviously, the old "seven dog years to one human year" theory is not exact. In puppyhood, a dog's year is actually comparable to more than seven human years, considering the puppy's rapid growth during his first year. Then, in adulthood, the ratio decreases. Regardless, the more viable rule of thumb is that the larger the dog, the shorter his expected lifespan. Of course, this can vary among individual dogs, with many living longer than expected, which we hope is the case and which often is the case in the Puli.

WHAT ARE THE SIGNS OF AGING?
By the time your dog has reached his senior years, you will know him very well, so the physical and behavioral changes that accompany aging should be

noticeable to you. Humans and dogs share the most obvious physical sign of aging: gray hair! Graying often occurs first on the muzzle and face, around the eyes. Other telltale signs are the dog's overall decrease in activity. Your older dog might be more content to nap and rest, and he may not show the same old enthusiasm when it's time to play in the yard or go for a walk. Other physical signs include significant weight loss or gain; more labored movement; skin and coat problems, possibly hair loss; sight and/or hearing problems; changes in toileting habits, perhaps seeming "unhousebroken" at times; and tooth decay, bad breath or other mouth problems.

There are behavioral changes that go along with aging, too. There are numerous causes for behavioral changes. Sometimes a dog's apparent confusion results from a physical change like diminished sight or hearing. If his confusion causes him to be afraid, he may act aggressively or defensively. He may sleep more frequently because his daily walks, though shorter now, tire him out. He may begin to experience separation anxiety or, conversely, become less interested in petting and attention.

There also are clinical conditions that cause behavioral changes in older dogs. One such condition is known as canine

SHADY PINES? NOT YET!
Is your Puli ready for the "old dogs' home"? If your dog has retained his energy and is in good shape (not overweight), you should consider yourself lucky. An active older dog who enjoys his food should not be changed to a senior food just because he is "of age." One of the super-premium adult foods (or even a growth or performance brand) might be a better choice for your feisty senior citizen. Every dog's condition and needs should be evaluated by his veterinarian. The correct diet for a senior provides the appropriate caloric density to maintain the body's condition as well as balanced nutrition.

cognitive dysfunction (familiarly known as "old-dog" syndrome). It can be frustrating for an owner whose dog is affected with cognitive dysfunction, as it can result

your senior dog, making more frequent trips to the vet if necessary and having bloodwork done to test for the diseases that can commonly befall older dogs.

This is not to say that, as dogs age, they all fall apart physically and become nasty in personality. The aforementioned changes are discussed to alert owners to the things that may happen as their dogs get older. Many hardy dogs remain active and alert well into old age. However, it can be frustrating and heartbreaking for

Don't force exercise on your senior Puli if he doesn't seem up to it. He'll let you know when he'd rather take it easy.

in behavioral changes of all types, most seemingly unexplainable. Common changes include the dog's forgetting aspects of the daily routine, such as times to eat, go out for walks, relieve himself and the like. Along the same lines, you may take your dog out at the regular time for a potty trip and he may have no idea why he is there. Sometimes a placid dog will begin to show aggressive or possessive tendencies or, conversely, a hyperactive dog will start to "mellow out."

Disease also can be the cause of behavioral changes in senior dogs. Hormonal problems (Cushing's disease is common in older dogs), diabetes and thyroid disease can cause increased appetite, which can lead to aggression related to food guarding. It's better to be proactive with

CAUSES OF CHANGE

Cognitive dysfunction may not be the cause of all changes in your older dog; illness and medication can also affect him. Things like diabetes, Cushing's disease, cancer and brain tumors are serious physical problems but can cause behavioral changes as well. Older dogs are more prone to these conditions, which should not be overlooked as possibilities for your dog's acting not like his "old self." Any significant changes in your senior's behavior are good reasons to take your dog to the vet for a thorough exam.

Your dog's reactions to medication can cause changes as well. The various types of corticosteroids are often cited as affecting a dog's behavior. If your vet prescribes any type of drug, discuss possible side effects before administering the medication to your dog.

owners to see their beloved dogs change physically and temperamentally. Just know that it's the same Puli under there, and that he still loves you and appreciates your care, which he needs now more than ever.

HOW DO I CARE FOR MY AGING DOG?

Again, every dog is an individual in terms of aging. Your dog might reach the estimated "senior" age for the Puli and show no signs of slowing down. However, even if he shows no outward signs of

While "old age" may be a relative term for your aging Puli, it is important to implement a senior-care program to ensure his good health.

> ### ACCIDENT ALERT!
> Just as we puppy-proof our homes for the new member of the family, we must accident-proof our homes for the older dog. You want to create a safe environment in which the senior dog can get around easily and comfortably, with no dangers. A dog that slips and falls in old age is much more prone to injury than an adult, making accident prevention even more important. Likewise, dogs are more prone to falls in old age, as they do not have the same balance and coordination that they once had. Throw rugs on hardwood floors are slippery and pose a risk; even a throw rug on a carpeted surface can be an obstacle for the senior dog. Consider putting down non-slip surfaces or confining your dog to carpeted rooms only.

aging, he should begin a senior-care program around seven or eight, or as recommended by the vet. He may not show it, but he's not a pup anymore! By providing him with extra attention to his veterinary care at this age, you will be practicing good preventive medicine, ensuring that the rest of your dog's life will be as long, active, happy and healthy as possible. If you do notice indications of aging, such as graying and/or changes in sleeping, eating or toileting habits, this is a sign to set up a senior-care visit with your vet right away to make sure that these changes are not related to any health problems.

SEPARATION ANXIETY AND SENIORS

As dogs are living longer, vets and behaviorists are paying more attention to care of the geriatric dog. One of the areas on which they focus is separation anxiety. This can occur in dogs of any age but, often, dogs who were never anxious about being left alone start to experience separation anxiety in old age. As the symptoms are displayed when the dog is alone, the condition can be hard to identify. However, if you start coming home to toilet accidents in the house or chewed-up furniture, separation anxiety is one likely cause.

In this case, your aging dog might do well if left crated while home alone for a few hours so that he can't engage in destructive behavior. This is also safer, as an older dog is less coordinated and may injure himself if left to roam freely. An item of clothing or other article bearing your scent may comfort him in his crate, along with some favorite toys. The crate should be well padded for his comfort and away from any drafts. If the dog has been crate-trained all his life, the crate will be a comforting safe haven for him. A word of warning: do not crate an older dog for more than three or four hours, as arthritic joints can worsen if the dog isn't given a chance to move around and stretch.

To start, senior dogs should visit the vet twice yearly for exams, routine tests and overall evaluations. Many veterinarians have special screening programs especially for senior dogs that can include a thorough physical exam; blood test to determine complete blood count; serum biochemistry test, which screens for liver, kidney and blood problems as well as cancer; urinalysis; and dental exams. With these tests, it can be determined whether your dog has any health problems; the results also establish a baseline for your pet against which future test results can be compared.

In addition to these tests, your vet may suggest additional testing, including an EKG, tests for glaucoma and other problems of the eye, chest x-rays, screening for tumors, blood pressure test, test for thyroid function and screening for parasites and reassessment of his preventive program. Your vet also will ask you questions about your dog's diet and activity level, what you feed and the amounts that you feed. This information, along with his evaluation of the dog's overall condition, will enable him to suggest proper dietary changes, if needed.

This may seem like quite a work-up for your pet, but veterinarians advise that older dogs need more frequent attention so that any health problems can be detected as early as possible. Serious conditions like kidney disease, heart disease and cancer may not present outward symptoms, or the problem may go undetected if the symptoms are mistaken by owners as just part of the aging process.

There are some conditions more common in elderly dogs that are difficult to ignore. Cognitive dysfunction shares much in common with senility and Alzheimer's disease, and dogs are not immune. Dogs can become confused and/or disoriented, lose their house-training, have abnormal sleep-wake cycles and interact differently with their owners. Be heartened by the fact that, in some ways, there are more treatment options for dogs with cognitive dysfunction than for people with similar conditions. There is good evidence that continued stimulation in the form of games,

play, training and exercise can help to maintain cognitive function. There are also medications (such as seligiline) and antioxidant-fortified senior diets that have been shown to be beneficial.

Cancer is also a condition more common in the elderly. While lung cancer, which is a major killer in humans, is relatively rare in dogs, almost all of the cancers seen in people are also seen in pets. If pets are getting regular physical examinations, cancers are often detected early. There are a variety of cancer therapies available today, and many pets continue to live happy lives with appropriate treatment.

Degenerative joint disease, often referred to as arthritis, is another malady common to both elderly dogs and humans. A lifetime of wear and tear on joints and running around at play eventually takes its toll and results in stiffness and difficulty in getting around. As dogs live longer and healthier lives, it is natural that they should eventually feel some of the effects of aging. Once again, if regular veterinary care has been available, your pet should not have been carrying extra pounds all those years and wearing those joints out before their time. If your pet was unfortunate enough to inherit hip dysplasia, osteochondritis dissecans or any of the other developmental orthopedic diseases, battling the onset of

WHAT A RELIEF!

Much like young puppies, older dogs do not have as much control over their excretory functions as they do as non-seniors. Their muscle control fades and, as such, they cannot "hold it" for as long as they used to. This is easily remedied by additional trips outside. If your dog's sight is failing, have the yard well lit at night and/or lead him to his relief site on lead. Incontinence should be discussed with your vet.

ADAPTING TO AGE

As dogs age and their once-keen senses begin to deteriorate, they can experience stress and confusion. However, dogs are very adaptable, and most can adjust to deficiencies in their sight and hearing. As these processes often deteriorate gradually, the dog makes adjustments gradually, too. Because dogs become so familiar with the layout of their homes and yards, and with their daily routines, they are able to get around even if they cannot see or hear as well. Help your senior dog by keeping things consistent around the house. Keep up with your regular times for walking and potty trips, and do not relocate his crate or rearrange the furniture. Your dog is a very adaptable creature and can make compensation for his diminished ability, but you want to help him along the way and not make changes that will cause him confusion.

degenerative joint disease was probably a longstanding goal. In any case, there are now many effective remedies for managing degenerative joint disease and a number of remarkable surgeries as well.

Aside from the extra veterinary care, there is much you can do at home to keep your older dog in good condition. The dog's diet is an important factor. If your dog's appetite decreases, he will not be getting the nutrients he needs. He also will lose weight, which is unhealthy for a dog at a proper weight. Conversely, an older dog's metabolism is slower and he usually exercises less, but he should not be allowed to become obese. Obesity in an older dog is especially risky, because extra pounds mean extra stress on the body, increasing his vulnerability to heart disease. Additionally, the extra pounds make it harder for the dog to move about.

You should discuss age-related feeding changes with your vet. For a dog who has lost interest in food, it may be suggested to try some different types of food until you find something new that the dog likes. For an obese dog, a "light"-formula dog food or reducing food portions may be advised, along with exercise appropriate to his physical condition and energy level.

As for exercise, the senior dog should not be allowed to become a "couch potato" despite his old age. He may not be able to handle the morning run, long walks and vigorous games of fetch, but he still needs to get up and get moving. Keep up with your daily walks, but keep the distances shorter and let your dog set the pace. If he gets to the point where he's not up for walks, let him stroll around the yard. On the other hand, many dogs remain very active in their senior years, so base changes to the exercise program on your own individual dog and what he's capable of. Don't worry, your Puli will let you know when it's time to rest.

Keep up with your grooming routine as you always have. Be extra-diligent about checking the skin and coat for problems. Older dogs can experience thinning coats as a normal aging process, but they can also lose hair as a result of medical problems. Some thinning is normal, but patches of baldness or the loss of significant amounts of hair is not.

Hopefully, you've been regular with brushing your dog's teeth throughout his life. Healthy teeth directly affect overall good health. We already know that bacteria from gum infections can enter the dog's body through the damaged gums and travel to the organs. At a stage in life when his organs don't function as well as they used to, you don't want anything to put additional strain on them. Clean teeth also contribute to a healthy immune system. Offering the dental-type chews in addition to toothbrushing can help, as they remove plaque and tartar as the dog chews.

Along with the same good care you've given him all of his life, pay a little extra attention to your dog in his senior years and keep up with twice-yearly trips to the vet. The sooner a problem is uncovered, the greater the chances of a full recovery.

AH, MY ACHING BONES!

As your pet ages and things that once were routine become difficult for him to handle, you may need to make some adjustments around the home to make things easier for your dog. Senior dogs affected by arthritis may have trouble moving about. If you notice this in your dog, you may have to limit him to one floor of the house so that he does not have to deal with stairs. If there are a few steps leading out into the yard, a ramp may help the dog. Likewise, he may need a ramp or a boost to get in and out of the car. Ensure that he has plenty of soft bedding on which to sleep and rest, as this will be comfortable for his aching joints. Also ensure that surfaces on which the dog walks are not slippery. Massaging his limbs, especially before he gets out of bed in the morning, is helpful too.

Investigate new dietary supplements made for arthritic dogs. Studies have found that products containing glucosamine added once or twice daily to the senior dog's food can have beneficial effects on the dog's joints. Many of these products also contain natural anti-inflammatories such as chondroitin, MSM and cetyl myristoleate, as well as natural herbal remedies and nutmeg. Talk to your vet about these supplements.

SHOWING YOUR

PULI

SHOW PREPARATION

Should you decide that you might try showing your Puli, then preparation cannot start too early. Accustom the youngster to standing still, as he will need to stay in the standing (or "stacked") position for the judge's evaluation and examination. Just a few minutes getting the dog used to having someone put his hands over the body, looking at the teeth, etc., are sufficient to begin. Training classes are a great help for your future show dog so that he will come to accept the approaches and handling of strangers. Talk to your Puli while he is being examined so that by the tone of your voice he feels reassured. It's very unfair to both the dog and the judge if the latter is expected to evaluate an upset animal and you blame the dog for reacting to a totally unfamiliar experience.

It's important that your Puli get used to having his dentition inspected, for a judge will wish to see that the teeth are correctly positioned and in good condition, and that the jaw closes properly. In the Puli, dogs not only need to have their teeth checked but must have their mouths inspected as well, since the standard requires a pigmented mouth.

Though the standard calls for a compact, well-balanced dog, this must be checked by a "hands-on" examination for proper construction, muscle tone, etc. A puppy must become accustomed to having a stranger feel his bones, spring of rib, loin, tail and other points. With the legs, the judge needs to get under the cords to

FOR MORE INFORMATION...

For reliable up-to-date information about registration, dog shows and other canine competitions, contact one of the national registries by mail or via the Internet.

American Kennel Club
5580 Centerview Dr., Raleigh, NC 27606-3390
www.akc.org

United Kennel Club
100 E. Kilgore Road, Kalamazoo, MI 49002
www.ukcdogs.com

Canadian Kennel Club
89 Skyway Ave., Suite 100, Etobicoke, Ontario
M9W 6R4, Canada
www.ckc.ca

The Kennel Club
1-5 Clarges St., Piccadilly, London W1Y 8AB, UK
www.the-kennel-club.org.uk

SHOW POTENTIAL

How possible is it to predict how your ten-week-old puppy will eventually do in the show ring? Most show dogs reach their prime at around three years of age, when their bodies are physically mature and their coats are in "full bloom." Experienced breeders, having watched countless pups grow into Best of Breed winners, recognize the glowing attributes that spell "show potential." When selecting a puppy for show, it's best to trust the breeder to recommend which puppy will best suit your aspirations. Some breeders recommend starting with a male puppy, which likely will be more "typey" than his female counterpart.

likely to test coats of show dogs for the use of artifice in presentation; therefore, if something like oil or lacquer has been used, it will soon be identified. Most owners will use some conditioner, perhaps in the form of lanolin, to prevent the cords from drying out too much. These preparations must be removed by careful bathing and rinsing before exhibiting. We normally trim around the feet to neaten them and tidy up the long cords that reach down on to the ground, so that the coat swings easily while moving. The cords of the tail, as naturally carried over the body, should merge with those of the body and hindlegs, so these tail cords may

find a good bend of stifle at the rear and a strong hock joint that does not flex forward.

The puppy must be trained to walk on a lead so that his gait can be evaluated in the show ring. When the Puli is moved, he is best seen trotting alongside his handler on a loose lead in order to show off his natural, light and springy action. There is no call to "string" the Puli up on a tight lead like a terrier. A tight lead will also cause the neck to be stretched in an unnatural manner and angle, which will affect the dog's natural action.

Preparation for show is not only ring training but also the coat and its presentation. Judges are

The author, Ann Arch, handling a young puppy bitch.

keep them from getting too dirty by looping the cords into bundles so that they are carried well above the ground and are less likely to become soiled or pick up debris. The bands used to hold the bundles should not be too tight or they will cut through the hair. We prefer the terrycloth bands, which are strong but gentle. Pre-show bathing varies from one dog and his coat type to the next. Some Pulik will need bathing several days before the show, while others can be bathed a day or so in advance.

THINKING ABOUT SHOWING?

Is dog showing in your blood? Are you excited by the idea of gaiting your handsome Puli around the ring to the thunderous applause of an enthusiastic audience? Are you

The author's daughter, Alexandra Davis, and her Puli, competing at a show in the UK and winning a Challenge Certificate.

also need reducing in length if they become too long.

A thorough bath and complete rinsing to ensure that the coat is natural will leave you with a very wet dog! We use old towels to absorb as much of the water as possible before using the dryer. The more water that can be wrung out, the quicker the drying time. The best time to work thoroughly through the whole coat is when the dog is practically dry, ensuring that all cords are separated right down to the skin level.

In our show dogs with full mature cords, we find it easiest to

BECOMING A CHAMPION

An official AKC championship of record requires that a dog accumulate 15 points under three different judges, including two "majors" under different judges. Points are awarded based on the number of dogs entered into competition, varying from breed to breed and place to place. A win of three, four or five points is considered a "major." The AKC annually assigns a schedule of points to adjust for variations that accompany a breed's popularity and the population of a given area.

- Does your puppy have any disqualifying faults?
- Is your Puli registered with the American Kennel Club?
- How much time do you have to devote to training, grooming, conditioning and exhibiting your dog?
- Do you understand the rules and regulations of a dog show?
- Do you have time to learn how to show your dog properly?
- Do you have the financial resources to invest in showing your dog?
- Will you show the dog yourself or hire a professional handler?
- Do you have a vehicle that can accommodate your weekend trips to the dog shows?

Success in the show ring requires more than a pretty face, a waggy tail and a pocketful of liver. Even though dog shows can be

Ch. Cordmaker Tennessee Waltz, imported from Australia, shown winning Best of Breed at the Westminster Kennel Club show in 2000, owned and handled by Carolyn Nusbickel.

Ch. Thunder Mount Cinkotai, a Top Ten Puli of the early 1980s, handled by breeder Augusta Plank to Best of Breed under judge Tom Stevenson at Rio Hondo Kennel Club in 1981.

certain that your beloved Puli is flawless? You are not alone! Every loving owner thinks that his dog has no faults, or too few to mention. No matter how many times an owner reads the breed standard, he cannot find any faults in his aristocratic companion dog. If this sounds like you, and if you are considering entering your Puli in a dog show, here are some basic questions to ask yourself:

- Did you purchase a "show-quality" puppy from the breeder?
- Is your puppy at least six months of age?
- Does the puppy exhibit correct show type for his breed?

exciting and enjoyable, the sport of conformation makes great demands on the exhibitors and the dogs. Winning exhibitors live for their dogs, devoting time and money to their dogs' presentation, conditioning and training. Very few novices, even those with good dogs, will find themselves in the winners' circle, though it does happen. Don't be disheartened, though. Every exhibitor began as a novice and worked his way up to the Group ring. It's the "working your way up" part that you must keep in mind.

Assuming that you have purchased a puppy of the correct type and quality for showing, let's

AKC GROUPS
For showing purposes, the American Kennel Club divides its recognized breeds into seven groups: Sporting Dogs, Hounds, Working Dogs, Terriers, Toys, Non-Sporting Dogs and Herding Dogs. The Puli is a Herding Dog.

begin to examine the world of showing and what's required to get started. Although the entry fee into a dog show is nominal, there are lots of other hidden costs involved with "finishing" your Puli, that is, making him a champion. Things like equipment, travel, training and conditioning

Author Ann Arch and daughter Alexandra Davis groom a Puli before showing.

all cost money. A more serious campaign will include fees for a professional handler, boarding, cross-country travel and advertising. Top-winning show dogs can represent a very considerable investment—over $100,000 has been spent in campaigning some dogs. (The investment can be less, of course, for owners who don't use professional handlers.)

Many owners, on the other hand, enter their "average" Pulis in dog shows for the fun and enjoyment of it. Dog showing makes an absorbing hobby, with many rewards for dogs and owners alike. If you're having fun, meeting other people who share your interests and enjoying the overall experience, you likely will catch the "bug." Once the dog-show bug bites, its effects can last a lifetime; it's certainly much better than a deer tick! Soon you will be envisioning yourself in the center ring at the Westminster Kennel Club Dog Show in New York City, competing for the prestigious Best in Show cup. This magical dog show is televised annually from Madison Square Garden, and the victorious dog becomes a celebrity overnight.

AKC CONFORMATION BASICS
Visiting a dog show as a spectator is a great place to start. Pick up the show catalog to find out what time your breed is being shown,

who is judging the breed and in which ring the classes will be held. To start, Pulik compete against other Pulik, and the winner is selected as Best of Breed by the judge. This is the procedure for each breed. At a group show, all of the Best of Breed winners go on to compete for Group One (first place) in their respective groups. For example, all Best of Breed winners in a given group compete against each other; this is done for all seven groups. The Puli competes in the Herding Group. Finally, all seven group winners go head to head in

MEET THE AKC
The American Kennel Club is the main governing body of the dog sport in the United States. Founded in 1884, the AKC consists of 500 or more independent dog clubs plus 4,500 affiliated clubs, all of which follow the AKC rules and regulations. Additionally, the AKC maintains a registry for pure-bred dogs in the US and works to preserve the integrity of the sport and its continuation in the country. Over 1,000,000 dogs are registered each year, representing over 150 recognized breeds. There are over 15,000 competitive events held annually for which over 2,000,000 dogs enter to participate. Dogs compete to earn over 40 different titles, from Champion to Companion Dog to Master Agility Champion.

ON THE MOVE

The truest test of a dog's proper structure is his gait, the way the dog moves. The American Kennel Club defines gait as "the pattern of footsteps at various rates of speed, each pattern distinguished by a particular rhythm and footfall." That the dog moves smoothly and effortlessly indicates to the judge that the dog's structure is well made. From the four-beat gallop, the fastest of canine gaits, to the high-lifting hackney gait, each breed varies in its correct gait; not every breed is expected to move in the same way. Each breed standard defines the correct gait for its breed and often identifies movement faults, such as toeing in, side-winding, over-reaching or crossing over.

the ring for the Best in Show award.

What most spectators don't understand is the basic idea of conformation. A dog show is often referred as a "conformation" show. This means that the judge should decide how each dog stacks up (conforms) to the breed standard for his given breed: how well does this Puli conform to the ideal representative detailed in the standard? Ideally, this is what happens. In reality, however, this ideal often gets slighted as the judge compares Puli #1 to Puli #2. Again, the ideal is that each dog is judged based on his merits in comparison to his breed standard, not in comparison to the other dogs in the ring. It is easier for judges to compare dogs of the same breed to decide which they think is the better specimen; in the Group and Best in Show ring, however, it is very difficult to compare one breed to another, like apples to oranges. Thus the dog's conformation to the breed standard—not to mention advertising dollars and good handling—is essential to success in conformation shows. The dog described in the standard (the standard for each AKC breed is written and approved by the breed's national parent club and then submitted to the AKC for approval) is the perfect dog of that breed, and breeders keep their eye on the standard when they choose which dogs to breed, hoping to get closer and closer to the ideal with each litter.

Another good first step for the novice is to join a dog club. You will be astonished by the many and different kinds of dog clubs in the country, with about 5,000 clubs holding events every year. Most clubs require that prospective new members present two letters of recommendation from existing members. Perhaps you've made some friends visiting a show held by a particular club and you would like to join that club. Dog clubs may specialize in a single breed, like a local or regional Puli club, or in a specific pursuit, such as obedience, tracking or herding events. There are all-breed clubs for all dog enthusiasts; they sponsor special training days, seminars on topics like grooming or handling or lectures on breeding or canine genetics. There are also clubs that specialize in certain types of dogs, like herding dogs, hunting dogs, companion dogs, etc.

A parent club is the national organization, sanctioned by the AKC, which promotes and safeguards its breed in the country. The Puli Club of America can be contacted on the Internet at www.puliclub.org. Membership information and an application are available online. The parent club holds an annual national

EXPRESS YOURSELF

The most intangible of all canine attributes, expression speaks to the character of the breed, attained by the combined features of the head. The shape and balance of the dog's skull, the color and position of the eyes and the size and carriage of the head mingle to produce the correct expression of the breed. A judge may approach a dog and determine instantly whether the dog's face portrays the desired impression for the breed, conveying nobility, intelligence and alertness among other specifics of the breed standard.

specialty show, usually in a different city each year, in which many of the country's top dogs, handlers and breeders gather to compete. At a specialty show, only members of a single breed are invited to participate. There are also group specialties, in which all members of a group are invited. For more information about dog clubs in your area, contact the AKC at www.akc.org on the Internet or write them at their Raleigh, NC address.

A show dog must be amenable to an all-over hands-on check by the judge, including an examination of his mouth and teeth.

OTHER TYPES OF COMPETITION

In addition to conformation shows, the AKC holds a variety of other competitive events. Obedience trials, agility trials and

FIVE CLASSES AT SHOWS

At most AKC all-breed shows, there are five regular classes offered: Puppy, Novice, Bred-by-Exhibitor, American-bred and Open. The Puppy Class is usually divided as 6 to 9 months of age and 9 to 12 months of age. When deciding in which class to enter your dog, whether male or female, you must carefully check the show schedule to make sure that you have selected the right class. Depending on the age of the dog, previous first-place wins and the sex of the dog, you must make the best choice. It is possible to enter a one-year-old dog who has not won sufficient first places in any of the non-Puppy Classes, though the competition is more intense the further you progress from the Puppy Class.

tracking trials are open to all breeds, while hunting tests, field trials, lure coursing, herding tests and trials, earthdog tests and coonhound events are limited to specific breeds or groups of breeds. The Junior Showmanship program is offered to aspiring young handlers and their dogs, and the Canine Good Citizen® Program is an all-around good-behavior test open to all dogs, pure-bred and mixed.

OBEDIENCE TRIALS

Any dog registered with the AKC, regardless of neutering or other disqualifications that would preclude entry in conformation competition, can participate in obedience trials. There are three levels of difficulty in obedience competition. The first (and easiest) level is the Novice, in which dogs can earn the Companion Dog (CD) title. The intermediate level is the Open level, in which the Companion Dog Excellent (CDX) title is awarded. The advanced level is the Utility level, in which dogs compete for the Utility Dog (UD) title. Classes at each level are further divided into "A" and "B," with "A" for beginners and "B" for those with more experience. In order to win a title at a given level, a dog must earn three "legs." A "leg" is accomplished when a dog scores 170 or higher (200 is a perfect score). The

scoring system gets a little trickier when you understand that a dog must score more than 50% of the points available for each exercise in order to actually earn the points. Available points for each exercise range between 20 and 40.

A dog must complete different exercises at each level of obedience. The Novice exercises are the easiest, with the Open and finally the Utility levels progressing in difficulty. Examples of Novice exercises are on- and off-lead heeling, a figure-8 pattern, performing a recall (or come), long sit, long down and standing for examination. In the Open level, the Novice-level exercises are required again, but this time without a leash and for longer durations. In addition, the dog must clear a broad jump, retrieve over a jump and drop on recall. In the Utility level, the

exercises are quite difficult, including executing basic commands based on hand signals, following a complex heeling pattern, locating articles based on scent discrimination and completing jumps at the handler's direction.

Once he's earned the UD title, a dog can go on to win the prestigious title of Utility Dog Excellent (UDX) by winning "legs" in ten shows. Additionally, Utility Dogs who win "legs" in Open B and Utility B earn points toward the lofty title of Obedience Trial Champion (OTCh.). Established in 1977 by the AKC, this title requires a dog to earn 100 points as well as three first places in a combination of Open B and Utility B classes under three different judges.

Ch. Jateko Bika of Pebbletree, a top winner of the 1980s, won Best of Breed and placed in the Herding Group at the AKC Centennial show in 1984.

Ch. Moonshadow Puttin On The Ritz, the number-one Puli for three years from 1989 to 1991, handled by Doug Holloway to Best in Show under judge Clint Harris at Langley Kennel Club in 1990.

Ch. Loakespark
Just Smart,
NAJ, lives up to
his name and
then some. At
home, he's just
Oliver.

AGILITY TRIALS

Agility trials became sanctioned by the AKC in August 1994, when the first licensed agility trials were held. Since that time, agility certainly has grown in popularity by leaps and bounds, literally! The AKC allows all registered breeds (including Miscellaneous Class breeds) to participate, providing the dog is 12 months of age or older. Agility is designed so that the handler demonstrates how well the dog can work at his side. The handler directs his dog through, over, under and around an obstacle course that includes jumps, tires, the dog walk, weave poles, pipe tunnels, collapsed tunnels and more. While working his way through the course, the dog must keep one eye and ear on the handler and the rest of his body on the course. The handler runs along with the dog, giving verbal and hand signals to guide the dog through the course.

Agility trials are a great way to keep your dog active, and they

Here's Oliver showing off his stuff at an agility trial.

will keep you running, too! You should join a local agility club to learn more about the sport. These clubs offer sessions in which you can introduce your dog to the various obstacles as well as training classes to prepare him for competition. In no time, your dog will be climbing A-frames, crossing the dog walk and flying over hurdles, all with you right beside him. Your heart will leap every time your dog jumps through the hoop—and you'll be having just as much (if not more) fun!

Oliver, weaving like a pro.

TRACKING TESTS

Tracking tests are exciting ways to test your Puli's instinctive scenting ability on a competitive level. All dogs have a nose, and all breeds are welcome in tracking tests. The first AKC-licensed tracking test took place in 1937 as part of the Utility level at an obedience trial, and thus competitive tracking was officially begun. The first title, Tracking Dog (TD), was offered in 1947, ten years after the first official tracking test. It was not until 1980 that the AKC added the title Tracking Dog Excellent (TDX), which was followed by the title Versatile Surface Tracking (VST) in 1995. Champion Tracker (CT) is awarded to a dog who has earned all three of those titles.

The TD level is the first and most basic level in tracking, progressing in difficulty to the TDX and then the VST. A dog must follow a track laid by a human 30 to 120 minutes prior in order to earn the TD title. The track is about 500 yards long and contains up to 5 directional changes. At the next level, the TDX, the dog must follow a 3- to 5-hour-old track over a course that is up to 1,000 yards long and has up to 7 directional changes. In the most difficult level, the VST, the track is up to five hours old and located in an urban setting.

HERDING EVENTS

The first recorded sheepdog trial was held in Wales in the late 19th century; since then, the popularity of herding events has grown around the world. The AKC began offering herding events in 1989, and participation

Ch. Prydain Trademark, the number-one Puli in 1998, with owner/handler Susan McConnell. Co-owner, Barbara Edwards.

is open to all breeds in the Herding Group as well as Rottweilers and Samoyeds. These events are designed to evaluate the dogs' herding instincts, and the aim is to develop these innate skills and show that herding dogs today can still perform the functions for which they were originally intended, whether or not they are actually used in working capacities. Herding events are designed to simulate farm situations and are held on two levels: tests and trials.

AKC herding tests are more basic than herding trials and are scored on a pass/fail system, meaning that dogs do not compete against each other to earn titles. Titles at this level are Herding Tested (HT) and the more difficult Pre-Trial Tested (PT). In addition, there is a non-competitive certification program, Herding Instinct Tested, which gives you a chance to evaluate the potential that your dog may have for herding. If your dog successfully passes this test, he receives a Herding Instinct Certificate, which makes him eligible to enter herding trials.

The more challenging herding trial level is competitive and requires more training and experience. There are three different courses (A, B and C, each with a different type of farm situation) with different types of livestock (cattle, sheep or ducks). There are three titles available on each course, Herding Started, Herding Intermediate and Herding Advanced, with each level being progressively more difficult. The type of livestock and course used for a dog is based on his breed's typical use. Once a Herding Advanced title has been earned on a course, the dog can then begin to strive for the Herding Champion title.

In addition to events held by the AKC, breed clubs often hold herding events for these breeds.

Other specialty organizations hold trials that are open to all herding breeds; the way these events are structured and the titles that are awarded differ from those of the AKC. For example, the American Herding Breed Association (AHBA) allows any breed with herding in its ancestry to participate, as well as allowing mixed-breed herding dogs. To pass the Herding Instinct Test, the handler works with the dog at the shepherd's direction while the shepherd evaluates the dog's willingness to approach, move and round up the sheep while at the same time following the instructions of his handler.

CANINE GOOD CITIZEN® PROGRAM

Have you ever considered getting your dog "certified"? The AKC's Canine Good Citizen® Program affords your dog just that opportunity. Your dog shows that he is a well-behaved canine citizen, using the basic training and good manners you have taught him, by taking a series of ten tests that illustrate that he can behave properly at home, in a public place and around other dogs. The tests are administered by participating dog clubs, colleges, 4-H clubs, Scouts and other community groups and are open to all pure-bred and mixed-breed dogs. Upon passing the ten tests, the suffix CGC is then applied to your dog's name.

At the competition level in AHBA events, dogs work with their handlers to move sheep up and down the field, through gates and into a pen, and also to hold the sheep without a pen, all while being timed. This is an amazing sight to see! A good dog working with the shepherd has to be the ultimate man-dog interaction. Rare breeds were often traditionally used for herding and, fortunately, the AHBA is more than happy to have rare breeds participate. Club members and spectators love to welcome some of these wonderful dogs that they have only read about but never seen.

The bond that you and your Puli will develop as you train for and participate in any arena of the dog sport is truly priceless.

My Puli

PUT YOUR PUPPY'S FIRST PICTURE HERE

Dog's Name _____

Date _____ Photographer _____